The 90s Club & the Secret of the Old Clock

Eileen Haavik McIntire

Amanita Books
Imprint of Summit Crossroads Press
Columbia, Maryland

The 90s Club & the Secret of the Old Clock

ISBN 978-0-9614519-0-5

Library of Congress Control Number: 2015916037

Cover design by Earthly Charms, earthlycharms.com.

Published by Amanita Books, imprint of Summit Crossroads Press, Columbia, MD, sumcross@aol.com. Contact the author at eileenmcintire@aol.com.

ACKNOWLEDGEMENTS

As I wrote this book, the BBC Network broadcast a news item about a woman who went skydiving on her one hundredth birthday. She proclaimed it an "exhilarating experience." Canoeing, dancing, running marathons and skydiving—what will ninety and one-hundred-year-olds do next?

The inspiration for this series came from meeting a woman at a pool party years ago. This woman was slim, attractive, the only one in the pool, and she was swimming laps. Later, I learned that she was ninety-one years old. Ninety-one!

Since then, I have collected articles about people in their nineties and one hundreds working, achieving, and challenging themselves along with the rest of us. That's why the slogan for the 90s Club series is "Able, Alert, and Active—Changing the paradigm for what it means to be ninety."

Like many upscale retirement complexes around the country, Whisperwood Retirement Village of the 90s Club series resembles a cruise ship with excellent meals served everyday and a pool, gym, classes, and activities of all sorts available to the residents.

My sincere thanks and appreciation to everyone who provided help and support with this and other books in the series. First, of course, is my husband, Dr. Roger McIntire, who writes practical books for parents. Many thanks also to Marilyn Magee, editor; Lorien Haavik, the White Oak Writers, especially Gale Deitch, long-time group leader, Ann Miller, and Dr. Tom Fowler; the Columbia Fiction Critique Group; and the participants in the late-lastnightbooks.com blog group.

- Eileen Haavik McIntire

CHAPTER 1

Nancy carried the two bags of groceries out to her car, refusing the offers of help that greeted her every step of the way. Really, she thought, you'd think I was over a hundred years old instead of just ninety. She tossed her head of short and curly white hair, but she had caught her reflection in the store's glass doors as she walked out and had to admit that she did look like an old lady. But I don't act or feel like one, she said to herself. After all, she had won the swing dance competition at Whisperwood Retirement Village just last Friday night.

She reached her new silver-tone Prius, opened the trunk, and lifted the bags into it. Then she closed the trunk and stepped back, looking up into the startled eyes of the man at the next car.

"Watch out!" he shouted, reaching for her arm.

"Get out of the way," another man yelled.

Nancy looked around in time to see a large sedan barreling towards her. Her mouth dropped open. Dumb with disbelief, she stepped back into the space between cars just before the sedan raced past. She watched the tail end of it exit the parking lot and speed down the road.

"Are you all right?" stuttered the man at the wheel of the next car. "I can't believe that happened."

"You could have been killed!" called out another man running towards them.

"Someone should call the police!" said a matronly woman in shorts and T-shirt pushing a stroller.

Nancy leaned against her car and caught her breath. She looked at the crowd around her and said in a quavering voice, "Did anyone see who it was? Get a license number?" They all shook their heads.

"I think it was dark blue. . . maybe black," said one of the bystanders. "A lot of mud plastered all over it. Hard to tell."

A young woman walked up to the group. "She needs to sit down." She looked at Nancy. "Let's go on over to the coffee shop. You must really be upset."

"I am," said Nancy, her voice weak. She was still trembling as she leaned on the young woman's arm. College student, Nancy guessed, seeing the long blonde hair, white T-shirt, and canvas backpack sagging with books, but she seemed more self-assured and competent than most of them.

"By the way, my name is Candace." She pulled a cell phone out of her jeans pocket. "I'll call the police."

"Don't bother," Nancy said, turning her thoughts to a car plastered with mud. That seemed like a deliberate attempt to obscure color and tag. She took a deep breath to make her voice stronger. "No one saw anything the police could use to catch him. I can't imagine what that driver was thinking. Going way too fast in a parking lot. Maybe he lost control."

"I don't think so." Candace cast her eyes over Nancy. "Are you all right?"

"If you wouldn't mind walking to the cafe with me," Nancy said. *Now I am acting like an old lady. Which I am not.* "I'm Nancy Dickenson." She gave Candace a tentative smile. "Thank you."

They stepped into the small cafe and sat at one of the round tables covered in white plastic that dotted the room. Windows with half curtains in a pastel flower pattern lined the front wall. The other walls were painted a pale blue. The place felt peaceful and relaxing. There were no other customers. Nancy glanced at Candace. A nice young woman who carried books. To Nancy, that was recommendation enough. Even if Candace had some ulterior motive, they were in a public place.

A server approached with menus. Nancy reached for the menu but found her hand shaking. Just a cup of tea," she said.

"Me too," added Candace, keeping her eyes on Nancy.

"Aren't you the private detective who lives at Whisperwood Retirement Village?" she asked. "The one who caught the criminals last year?"

Nancy fluttered her hand. "Not just me. The 90s Club, all of us together."

"My mother works there," said Candace. "She told me all about it, but you wouldn't know her. She's a nurse in the Alzheimer's Unit in another building."

Nancy barely heard Candace. She tried to remember exactly what happened. Had it been her fault? Stepping out into the path of a car? But no, she didn't think so. She managed a smile at the server as she delivered their tea and withdrew, then looked at Candace. "What did you mean before, when you said you didn't think it was an accident?"

"I was walking towards you, heading to the store and just happened to notice the car behind you waiting with the engine running and blocking the parked cars." She glanced at her teacup and reached for the sugar packets. "I thought it was just sitting there while someone ran into the store to get something." She tore open the packets and dumped the sugar into her tea.

"I remember passing it," said Nancy, nodding her head. "Saw it. Didn't pay any attention."

Candace picked up her cup. "It was waiting for you. When you were in a vulnerable position back of your car, it went for you. That was premeditated and deliberate." She took a sip. "It was coming in my direction but passed too fast for me to make out the tag number in back. Anyway, mud was splashed across it."

Nancy frowned. Candace was right. Premeditated and deliberate. "What about the color? Make?"

"Should have noted the make, but by that time, I was concerned about you."

"You are very observant," Nancy said. "Could you see who was driving the car?"

Candace shook her head. "Tinted windows. It all happened so fast, and I was looking for the tag number."

Nancy took a deep breath. "I can't imagine why anyone would go after me like that. The trouble at Whisperwood was over with last summer, and we caught the bad guys. Nothing suspicious going on now," she smiled at Candace, "that I know of." But that was the problem, wasn't it? Someone considered her a threat. What kind of skullduggery were they up to at Whisperwood that they needed her out of the way?

"That driver must have had a reason." Candace echoed Nancy's thoughts as she folded her arms on the table. "Just a fluke you survived." She flicked her eyes across Nancy's face. "How do you feel now. Any better?"

Nancy picked up her tea cup, relieved to find her hand steady. "I think I'm all right."

Candace placed a hand on Nancy's arm. "But you have to drive back up the mountain to Whisperwood. That's a long, lonely road, and he might have something else planned." She snapped her fingers. "I'll tell you what. I'll follow you. It won't take long, and I'll feel better knowing you're safe." She waved at the window. "Nice day for a drive anyway."

"That's such an imposition," Nancy began, as she assessed Candace and her story. She seemed like a nice young woman. Probably was.

"I won't take no for an answer."

***

Leave the Driving to Us!

Whisperwood's shuttle bus takes residents to town for shopping at the grocery store and the mall every Monday, Wednesday, and Friday, departing Whisperwood at 10 a.m. and 1 p.m. The shuttle departs from town at 12 noon and 5 p.m.

Leave your car at home and use this convenient and safe service instead. Contact the Transportation Department for more information on Whisperwood's airport shuttle.

-The Whisperwood Breeze, Newsletter of Whisperwood Retirement Village

CHAPTER 2

That night at dinner in Whisperwood's spacious dining room, Nancy turned her close call into a light misadventure as she recounted the episode to her 90s Club friends. Nancy, Louise Owens, and George Burroughs founded the club at Whisperwood Retirement Village almost a year ago when they all turned ninety.

"You could have been killed!" Louise said, flicking her long gray braid. Fitz Connelly, also a club member and the fourth at their table, nodded in agreement.

"Why would anyone go after you?" asked George, sitting back with his hands across his stomach. Tonight he wore a neon green polo shirt with periwinkle blue slacks. "Are you detecting again?"

Nancy shrugged and ignored her fears. No use getting everyone upset. "It was probably some yahoo who had drunk too much beer. Let's forget about it."

"What about that woman, Candace?" asked Fitz in his Jamaican accent. "She could have been one of them."

Louise looked up. "Long blonde hair? Mother works in the Alzheimer's Unit?"

Nancy nodded. 'She mentioned that."

"She's all right. Helps out over there." Louise picked up a forkful of green beans. "Friendly. Met her when I visited Molly. Such a sad case." She knocked on wood.

Nancy knew Molly's story. A sad case indeed. "I thought Candace was all right. Carried a backpack full of books."

Fitz laughed. "Recommendation enough."

With some grumbling from George, the foursome put the subject aside and tackled their meals.

The parking lot episode had rattled Nancy. The next day, she still felt so unsettled that she spent a leisurely morning sipping tea while reading a travel brochure and musing about a summer trip.

Suddenly, angry shouts from the hall outside her apartment interrupted the morning peace. "Never, never, never!" a woman yelled. A door slammed.

Nancy listened. Her huge fawn-colored cat Malone pricked up his ears, hunched down, and stared at the door.

Which neighbor was it? What did the woman mean? Never what? Nancy glanced at her watch. Ten a.m. Malone jumped off the window sill, stretched, and walked regally to the hall door to sniff under it.

Nancy watched him cross the room, but her eyes stopped at the innocent-appearing white envelope on the dining room table. The envelope was addressed to her in a graceful hand and it leaned upright against a vase. She had placed it that way to remind her to reply—as if she could ever forget it. She frowned as an icy shiver of uncertainty crept down her back.

The letter had arrived in the mail two days earlier. The return address said Morgantown. Nancy had opened the envelope eagerly, expecting news from a friend who lived there. She laughed with grim humor. She had not expected the letter to change her life and the memories she cherished of her beloved Bill.

She tossed her head and turned to stare out the window in an attempt to shake off the devastating news delivered so innocently. She would not think about that letter now. She hitched up the sleeves of her black turtleneck and went back to reading the brochure while listening for what might happen next down the hall.

The next minute she threw down the brochure and sat up in disbelief. She retrieved the brochure and reread it.

The first part was an enticing description of a sedate bus trip through Maine and Nova Scotia. Exactly what she wanted. But in fine print at the bottom an age limit was set forth. Age limit!

Nancy couldn't believe her eyes and she read for a third time the offending line: "Participants limited to able-bodied seniors under seventy-five." The tour planners had selected the arbitrary age of seventy-five? Some kind of insurance or liability concern? Ridiculous. If the trip was strenuous, say so. Let the customer decide and sign a waiver. Everyone had to sign waivers anyway. An accident could happen to anyone.

Nancy fumed as she stepped to the phone to call her friend Louise, paraphrasing a quote from Shakespeare in her mind: "I am ninety, if you prick me do I not bleed? If you tickle me do I not laugh? If you poison me do I not die? And if you wrong me shall I not revenge?" The last line would do well for Louise: This was just the kind of arbitrary discrimination Louise loved to fight. She had hesitated about going on such a trip. This bit of age discrimination might push her over the line, and Nancy would like the company.

Before she could get to the phone, someone knocked on the door. She tossed the brochure on the table and shooed Malone into the bedroom. He was not a nice kitty cat. He was arrogant and feisty and made his feelings known through his sharp claws. Nancy suspected he was the abandoned offspring of a bobcat. He would take advantage of any opportunity to escape and stalk the residents in the long halls of Whisperwood Retirement Village.

Nancy liked Whisperwood; she liked living on top of a wooded mountain in central West Virginia, and she was close to celebrating one year there. She still got depressed sometimes late at night, but the activities and her friends at Whisperwood kept the nightmares at bay most of the time. She didn't want Malone to scare anyone away.

She opened the door. Two gray-haired women stood in the hall. One was tall, youthful-looking and African-American. She smiled at Nancy. The shorter, heavy-set one clutched a potted geranium in her fat pink fingers.

"Ms. Dickenson? We've only met briefly," the short one said in a soft southern drawl, "but my husband and I moved in about six months ago. We got a good deal because they were still renovating the place." She thrust the plant at Nancy. "Grace Maury."

She brushed her hands on her creased navy slacks. The crisp, white, button-down shirt and slacks suggested a retired business woman. Nancy remembered seeing the names "Grace and Richard Maury" on a door down and across the hall. She had wondered what kind of people would display a vase of Dollar Store plastic flowers on their hall shelf. Every apartment had such a shelf in the hall beside the door for mementos and treats the residents wanted to share. But cheap plastic flowers?

"A belated thank you for saving Whisperwood last year," Grace added, sneaking a look past Nancy into the apartment.

Nancy nodded and took the plant with a smile. "Not just me. The 90s Club did that. I'm glad you stopped by. Come on in. I've seen you in the hall and was looking for an excuse to meet you."

The slim, black woman followed Grace. She kept a relaxed posture with her left hand in her pants pocket, but put forth the other one. "I'm Betts Horner. I was visiting Grace and came along to meet you." Her well-fitted jeans and red sweater made her seem younger than her gray hair implied. She took long steps and her manner was quiet but brusque. She looked at Nancy out of shrewd eyes, her head cocked like an alert terrier's. Nancy looked back with a smile, recognizing in Betts a woman used to being in charge, even though she seemed to be deferring to Grace at the moment.

"I'm so pleased to meet you both," Nancy said. She turned to Betts. "You've lived here awhile, though, haven't you? I've seen you in the dining room."

"Almost three years. I've seen you, too." Betts' smile lit up her face. "Heard so much about you. Thrilled to actually meet you at last." Her smile widened to a grin. "A real live detective. Fancy that." Her words carried a touch of irony. Nancy wondered what that meant.

"I'm retired, you know," said Nancy. "I'm pleased you stopped by."

Nancy ushered them into the living room, casting an eye over the geranium. "Thank you for the plant. It's so cheerful." She hoped Malone wouldn't eat it. Were geraniums poisonous? She swept a hand across the credenza to push the dust aside and set the plant down next to the square-faced mantle clock. She turned to her guests. "Would you like some tea?"

"Tea would be delightful," said Grace, casting her eyes around the room. They rested for a moment on the computer.

Betts nodded. "Love it."

"Take a seat," said Nancy, waving a hand at the couch. "I can talk to you from the kitchen." A loud snarl issued from the bedroom.

Betts jumped. "Wow! Is that the fearsome wildcat I've heard about?"

Nancy laughed. "Don't worry about him. I shut him in the bedroom. He isn't good around strangers."

That wasn't the half of it, she thought, but he had saved her life and the lives of her friends a year ago, so no one who knew the story complained about him any more. Nancy just thought it would be better if there was no reason to complain.

"You're probably wondering why we're here," said Betts, removing a stack of newspapers on the couch to clear a place to sit. Grace followed Nancy into the kitchen, lifting an eyebrow and sniffing at the clutter.

Nancy noticed Grace's reaction with amusement. She had grown up with a housekeeper who took care of the dusting and cleaning. As a result, Nancy had no interest in housework and never learned the knack. Nor did she have interior decorating skills. The furniture was plain and practical, the couch having a wood frame and beige cushions with a simple wood coffee table in front of it. The two chairs were a modern Scandinavian design. Only the souvenirs of previous cases resting on the credenza and bookcase would provoke any interest.

Grace peered at an unlabeled jar on the counter. "Oh, good, this is honey, isn't it?"

Nancy glanced at the jar and nodded. "I'm well supplied, now that my friend Louise has taken up beekeeping here." She took the jar and set it on a tray along with a bowl of sugar. "Too early in the spring to take honey, but her beekeeping friends are happy to share from last year."

Grace's eyes lit up. "Gracious, how wonderful. I collect honey from all over everyplace." She opened a cupboard and peered in but quickly closed it as cans threatened to cascade out onto the counter.

Nancy turned away to hide a smile. Yes, she was a terrible housekeeper—even with kitchen cupboards. Still, the fact that Grace collected honey was interesting. Must come from a farming background. More to Grace than met the eye.

Grace laughed. "Better be careful with that cupboard. Almost started an avalanche. Anyway, my daddy kept bees himself. Maybe I can help your friend. That's Louise Owens, isn't it? The one with the long braid down her back?"

"Yes, the braid." Sometimes Louise flicked that braid around so much, Nancy wanted to take a knife to it. "I'll let her know. I'm sure she could use some help."

She took three cups of water out of the microwave, put them on the tray and added tea bags.

Grace picked up the jar of honey and sniffed it with the air of a connoisseur. "Maybe pine pollen honey. Dark. Tasty. One of my favorites." She carried it with her as she followed Nancy into the living room.

"I heard that." Betts laughed. "Along with apple blossom, avocado, fireweed, tupelo, and all those other honeys you rave about." She winked at Nancy as she picked up the newspapers on the coffee table and set them on the floor.

"Tupelo's the best. No question." Grace waved her hand. "Anyway, catch more flies with honey than vinegar."

"I am not interested in catching flies," retorted Betts.

Nancy set the tray on the coffee table. "Here you go. It's English Breakfast, which is all I have." All she liked, actually. She handed a cup to Grace and then to Betts.

Grace poured a dollop of honey in her tea. "Delightful," said Grace, tasting the tea on her tongue. "Just what I thought. Pine pollen." Betts rolled her eyes.

Nancy turned to Betts. "So you've been here three years. You must like it here. I certainly do."

"Better than I thought at first," said Betts, "considering it's in the middle of West Virginia. At least West Virginia was Union country." She sipped the tea. "I'm descended from slaves, but they escaped to Philadelphia. Still hold a grudge though."

Nancy glanced at her. Betts wasn't joking, not that slavery was anything to joke about, but the statement was odd as a conversation starter.

"I just love Whisperwood. Best of two worlds," added Grace. "Town living in the country."

Nancy smiled. "I usually compare it to a cruise ship. I do like the woods and the landscaping too."

"Don't forget the meals we don't have to cook." Grace added. She took another sip of tea. "I want to apologize for the scene this morning. Embarrassing. I'm sure everyone on this hall heard it."

Betts leaned back and watched Grace with a raised eyebrow. "Short temper this one," she said, flashing another smile at Nancy. "We hope you weren't upset by the shouting and the door slamming. Grace works hard, yes she does, to be quite amiable."

"Unless provoked," Grace added, frowning down at her cup. "Nobody takes advantage of me. Nobody."

"Didn't bother me," said Nancy, "although I did wonder. . ."

"Anyway, I wanted to ask you about a problem I have," interrupted Grace, putting her teacup down. "When I heard about you being such a great detective, I got real excited 'cause I need help with a puzzle and a pest."

Nancy's eyes began to sparkle. "A puzzle and a pest?" So that's what the shouting was all about. "This sounds intriguing. Tell me about it."

"I inherited an old clock that's been in the family for generations—since before the war, in fact. War Between the States, that is. I own it—no question about that." Grace's voice was firm, and she looked Nancy in the eye.

"Now comes the pest part," laughed Betts.

"My cousin wants it." Grace wrinkled her nose in distaste. "My gun-collecting, reenactment buff, Civil War proud cousin wants it, says it's his and I should give it to him. Never. The nerve."

"So you've had it a long time," said Nancy cautiously, resorting to reflective listening. "It must mean a lot to you."

Grace peered at Nancy over the teacup. "That's not the only reason I'm keeping it."

Betts sat up with a smile and crossed her arms. "Now we're getting to it."

Grace frowned. "It contains a puzzle, too, a family secret I can't figure out."

Nancy recognized Grace's attempt to act casual about something that must mean a great deal to her, daring Nancy to make fun of her problem. "What kind of puzzle?" she asked.

"I don't know. Whatever it is has to do with the Civil War." Grace shrugged. "My family's from Richmond, Virginia. Old South. But my side of the family never did agree with the southern cause. Brother against brother, you know. I mean, how can you justify slavery or fighting to keep it? We were abolitionists. Kept that bit secret. Had to, in those parts."

Betts snorted. "They didn't want to get lynched, but lynching was okay for my people."

Grace frowned at her. "That's why I go ahead and call it the Civil War or War Between the States. My other relatives still call it the War of Northern Aggression. Ridiculous."

"I'm not a southerner," said Betts, sitting up straight. "My great, great grandmother escaped out of Virginia and made it to Philadelphia. That's where I'm from. Philadelphia."

Nancy glanced at her, then looked back at Grace. "What makes you think there's some kind of puzzle connected with the old clock?"

"Family legend." Grace twisted her hands and grimaced. "Which I wouldn't care one whit about if my cousin wasn't so hell-bent on getting the clock away from me. He's the most self-serving man I ever met. Why does he want the clock?"

"Wouldn't it be a valuable antique?" Nancy asked.

Grace laughed and got up to pace the floor, her hands clasped behind her back. "You might think so to hear me talk. Maybe it is worth something, maybe it's worth a lot. Probably so, but he'd have to pay me what it's worth—and you can bet I'd check that out—so there'd be no profit in it for him. Got to be something else. That's another reason why I think there's more to that clock and," she looked at Nancy, "that's why I say there's a puzzle connected to it."

Betts laughed, waving her tea cup. "Maybe Jefferson Davis or Robert E. Lee or some other Confederate big gun wound it up one day."

"This is serious, Betts. I'm afraid of that man and what he might do." Grace turned to Nancy. "You like puzzles, Nancy. Everyone here says you do. I'd like you to come over to my apartment and take a look at it. What do you say? Will you do that? Just look at it, that's all I ask."

Nancy sat back, surprised. She swept her eyes across her living room, skipping past the white envelope and stopping at the square-faced mantel clock resting on the credenza next to the geranium. It was a relic from a case she'd solved long ago. The memory made her smile. She was curious. An old clock with a secret. How could she resist that?

"It's fairly large," said Betts, "and quite pretty. Porcelain case covered in paste flowers."

"It's not a big ol' grandfather clock," added Grace. "My ancestors had a jewelry store, back even before the civil war. They kept the clock in the window. Public service, you know, since there weren't so many clocks or watches around then." She hesitated. "At least that's what my folks told me." She sat down with a thump and picked up the teacup.

Nancy looked at Grace, her hands tense around the teacup, watching Nancy with such hope in her eyes.

A puzzle in an old clock. How intriguing. She was curious—people said too curious—and her curiosity took her down strange pathways. She was lucky she'd survived so far. A memory of the car bearing down on her flashed through her mind. She set down her cup. "Let's take a look at it," she said.

***

Appraisal Fair Next Saturday!

Do you have an antique and wonder just how valuable it is? Bring it to Whisperwood's annual Appraisal Fair. Auctioneer and appraiser Buck Wilson has again volunteered to share his expertise with us. He will be in the lobby from 9 a.m. until noon. Appraisals will be done on a first come, first served basis. Cost: $10/item. All proceeds to benefit the college scholarship fund for our talented senior high school students who serve us faithfully every day.

- The Whisperwood Breeze, Newsletter for Whisperwood Retirement Village

CHAPTER 3

Grace led the way to her apartment down the hall. As Nancy and Betts waited for Grace to open the door, Maria Schmidt hobbled towards them on her walker. Her teal pants were too loose and too short, and the striped blue blouse looked more like a pajama top. Nancy tried to hide behind Betts, hoping Maria wouldn't see her and cursing her luck that Maria would choose this time to creep by. What was she doing here anyway? She didn't live down this hall.

Maria stopped to chat, pulled at Betts' sleeve, and exposed Nancy. "What a coincidence," she exclaimed, her German accent changing the W to V. "Nancy, I was just coming to see you."

Of course. Nancy smiled noncommittally. What did the woman want now? Nancy usually avoided her, not having the patience to deal with Maria's bizarre opinions. Her insistence that the United States started World War II was only one example. Everyone at Whisperwood had listened to her story. No arguments or facts could dissuade her. "American fighter planes bombed my village in Germany and destroyed everything. The war was their fault and that is why"—here she would gaze triumphantly at her listeners—"I refuse to become an American citizen." But she remained in America to collect her Social Security and pension checks.

Her eyes were blue, and she kept her hair blonde. She must have been attractive once, but now she looked dumpy and frail and after several encounters at the bridge tables, Nancy found Maria a bit dull and couldn't help feeling impatient. She did not want to get involved in Maria's multiple problems.

"I'm busy right now," Nancy said, "maybe I'll see you later."

After a brief smile, Maria ignored the other two women standing in the open doorway. "I don't know what to do, Nancy." She dabbed at her eyes with a tissue. "My grandson. Michael, you know. I just get call from him. How was I to know he was in Mexico? Nobody tells me nothing. And now they arrest him and he needs money. I don't understand. How could this happen?"

"Arrested?" said Nancy. "Are you sure?"

"He just called me." Maria began to cry. "He is in some dirty Mexican jail and says I should wire him $5,000 so he can pay bail and leave. He say he didn't do nothing. They just arrest him for nothing! Where do I get $5,000? How do I wire him if I get such money?" She reached for Nancy's hand. "What can I do? He insist I not call his parents."

"He says he needs money and sounded like your grandson." Nancy shook her head. Even she, with no sons or grandsons, had gotten those calls. Maria was a made-to-order victim. "How do you know it was your grandson?"

Maria clasped her hands as if in prayer. Nancy was in no doubt she was terrified. "Of course it was Michael. He tell me his name. Who else would know such a thing?"

Nancy knew how that worked. Maria had probably heard a young man's voice and asked, "Michael, is that you?" Easy for him to pick up from there. She patted Maria's arm reassuringly. "All right. The first thing you do is call his parents and find out where he is. My bet is that he's home or at school. He is certainly not in

Mexico." Nancy held up her hand as Maria began to object. "It's a scam, Maria. Your grandson is all right. Go call his folks."

"A. . .a scam? You mean a trick?" Maria leaned on her walker as relief flooded her face. "Of course. I call his parents at once." She gripped Nancy's hand and squeezed it. "Thank you. You must be right. Why would he be in Mexico? Why would he be arrested? He is a good boy." She hobbled back down the hall.

"I get scam calls all the time," said Nancy, shaking her head as she watched Maria, "and ignore them. I don't pick up the phone unless I recognize the caller."

"Sure" added Betts. "It ain't rude to be shrewd."

"Just because you don't recognize the caller doesn't mean it's a scam," said Grace, bustling into her apartment. "Could be legitimate and it could be good news. I got a call once and found out I won a cruise. Promotional stunt but a cruise is a cruise. I enjoyed it. You never can tell."

"Scary, more like, though," added Betts, opening the door wider and ushering Nancy into the apartment. "I've gotten a couple of those calls here. Not too many, but they seemed to know a lot about me. That's what surprises me."

"Are you sure they didn't just lead you on, picking up on something you said?" In Nancy's experience, some of those callers were astute, like the one who called Maria.

"I'm savvy about that kind of thing." Betts folded her arms as she spoke. "But I've talked to other people here, and they agree, that is, the smart ones do. The callers know a little too much about us for the call to be random from a telephone directory. I've contacted the Attorney General's Office in Charleston."

Grace drew a quick breath and looked at Betts. "You have? Is it really that much of a problem? I hang up on them. No big deal."

"Glad you called the state," said Nancy. "Those con artists prey on us seniors. You saw how scared Maria was. They can be vicious."

"Yes, good thing to do." Grace smiled and patted Betts on the back. "Betts is sharp about stuff like that," she said, "but I really don't think anyone here would do such a thing. Those scammers call everybody, and they're probably in India or some place."

Nancy paused in the foyer and looked around. Unlike her own apartment, Grace's was uncarpeted with light oak flooring. Two wicker chairs and a wicker love seat matched the blond floor color and the cushions were covered in red-flowered fabric. The red flower design was repeated in two area rugs. A large ficus tree and a smaller palmetto stood near the windows in the late-morning sunshine. Out of curiosity, Nancy walked over and felt the leaves. Fabric with plastic stems. Even so, the room felt pleasant—and tropical. Way south, thought Nancy with a grin.

"I'll get the clock," Grace said as she hurried into a back room.

"That clock," Betts walked over to a wicker chair and sat down, "is more trouble than it's probably worth. It's pretty, though. I'd buy it and make a profit on e-Bay if Grace wanted to sell."

Grace returned, carrying a bundle wrapped in a towel. From the way Grace bent over to carry the clock in both arms, Nancy guessed it must be heavy. Grace set the clock on the dining room table and slipped off the towel.

Nancy leaned forward to take a close look. The clock was close to two feet high with bouquets of pale pink and blue porcelain flowers decorating the white porcelain case. The hands and numerals on the face were black against a white background.

"What did I tell you, Nancy?" said Betts, lounging sideways in the chair. She'd hooked her arm over the back. "Too feminine for my taste and where would you hide a secret?"

Nancy ran her fingers across the delicate porcelain flowers.

"The trim is gold leaf," she said. "Exquisite." She studied the front, then turned it around to look at the back. A cursory glance yielded no revelations. "This will require some time and study." She looked over the clock at Grace. "Would you mind if I took it back to my apartment for a few days?"

"I guess not." Grace cast a fond look at the clock. "You wouldn't mind signing a receipt for it, would you?"

A receipt? The question stunned Nancy for a moment. She was just making a friendly gesture of help, but she didn't mind signing a receipt if that's what Grace wanted. Put it on a business-like basis even if the business was free. What could the puzzle be? The question intrigued her.

"No need for a receipt," said Betts. "I'm a witness that you're borrowing the clock from Grace for study. Simple."

Grace laughed. "Sorry. I forget myself. In business too long, I guess. Of course you can take the clock for a few days. Jefferson will never imagine you have it, Nancy. I'm afraid the next thing he's going to try is to break in and steal it from me." She put her hands on her hips. "Or wheedle it out of Richard, that damn fool." She glanced at them and laughed. "My husband. As usual, he's out on the golf course."

"The locks on our hall doors are so flimsy it's ridiculous." Betts sniffed and frowned at the front door.

Nancy studied the clock. What could the puzzle be? She looked up at Grace. "Does the clock work?"

"I think so. I just haven't wound it in months. Kept it hidden away." Grace reached around to a recess in the back and pulled out a key. She inserted it into the mechanism and wound the clock. It began ticking. Grace grinned. "Yep. It works."

Someone knocked on the door. Grace looked from Betts to Nancy. "Jefferson," she said, covering the clock and returning it to the bedroom. Betts walked to the door, opened it and stepped aside to allow the tall statesmanlike figure in the hall to walk in. He swung a gold-knobbed glistening mahogany cane. With his bushy white hair and white mustache, he resembled the Mark Twain look-alikes Nancy had seen at book festivals.

She supposed he worked at the image. He ignored Betts, who made a face at his back, and bowed to Nancy. "And who is this lovely creature?" he asked in a soft southern voice. Perhaps not Mark Twain, then. Perhaps a southern plantation owner. Nancy could almost smell magnolia blossoms. She winced at his words. At ninety years old, she was no one's lovely creature any more. This would-be charmer must be Jefferson.

Grace returned from the bedroom. "This is our neighbor, Nancy Dickenson. We've just met. Nancy, this is my cousin Jefferson Topham."

The man's shrewd eyes raked Nancy up and down. "Ah yes, the detective. Pleased to meet you, my dear." He turned to Grace. "My name is Jefferson *Lee* Topham. I'll thank you to remember that. It's a proud name."

Grace waved that aside. "What do you want?"

"I came by to apologize for our slight misunderstanding this morning and ask you to join me for supper tonight." He glanced at his watch. "We'll meet you at five, early enough to beat the crowds. We are cousins and should get to know each other better."

Grace folded her arms. "Betts comes too."

Jefferson glanced at Betts. "I'm afraid not," said Jefferson. "We'll be meeting another couple. No room for an extra." Then he turned to Nancy. "Unless you'd like to come, Miss Dickenson."

Nancy stared at him, open-mouthed. How appallingly rude. She struggled to find an appropriate response. Finally she spluttered, "No, thank you. I have plans." She glanced at Betts, who stood with arms folded by the back wall, an unreadable expression on her face.

"Then I'm sorry I can't come. I also have plans." Grace walked him to the door and opened it. Nancy watched her put her hand on his back and push. He stepped out into the hall, turned, and bowed to them. "Perhaps some other time. . ." Grace closed the door in his face.

Nancy turned to Betts. "I can't believe that guy. I'm so sorry."

"Forget it." Betts shrugged as Grace hugged her.

"He will never get that clock," Grace said through gritted teeth.

Nancy returned to her apartment, carrying the clock still swaddled in the towel in both arms. It was heavy. She unwrapped it and set it on her bedroom dresser. After meeting Jefferson, she decided to set it up in the privacy of her bedroom away from the prying eyes of any visitors. That would be more secure than on the living room credenza. She studied the clock and when the phone rang, she answered it absentmindedly without checking the caller ID, but she recognized the voice. Maria Schmidt.

"You were right, Nancy," said Maria, speaking in shrill, excited tones. "It was a spam."

"Scam," corrected Nancy, rolling her eyes.

"Scam, then." Maria paused. "I call my son and my grandson, he answer. Michael, you know. He was not in Mexico. Not ever. All big mistake." She laughed. "Thank you so much. Such relief, I can't tell you. Thank you, thank you."

"Good. That's fine then." Nancy hung up. But how much of a mistake was it? Everyone Nancy knew had been approached by one scam operator or another, especially if they had a computer. Fortunately, most people knew better than to fall for the Nigerian prince or general with millions he wanted to send you if he only had your bank account number. But new schemes popped up all the time.

Bad people. Thinking of bad people reminded her of Jefferson

Lee Topham. How dare he insult Betts like that. Most people at Whisperwood were kind, accepting, and tolerant. He was not and with luck might move on to somewhere else. Meanwhile, she would make every effort to include Grace and Betts in her own circle of friends as well as the 90s Club. She didn't think either one was close to ninety yet, but they were still welcome. In fact, Nancy's personal policy was to welcome everyone, but some people were more difficult than others.

She knew it was Whisperwood's policy too, with one caveat. You had to be able to afford to live at Whisperwood, and Whisperwood was not cheap. The people here had money, and that made it an attractive proposition for a scam artist.

***

Nancy joined the bridge club meeting after lunch that day. Her friends and fellow 90s Club members, Louise, George, and Fitz, were regulars, too. Unlike other bridge groups where misplays could ruin friendships, players laughed at their mistakes and listened to the latest gossip as play commenced around the tables.

This time, Nancy heard Betts' name and turned to see who had mentioned it. Nancy had met the woman before. What was her name? Bianca, wasn't it? A stout Hispanic woman whose middle-aged children had paid for her apartment at Whisperwood and often visited her. Her friendly outgoing personality made her welcome in most groups, and she often joined in the activities offered at Whisperwood, including the bridge classes. She was quite a good player now. Nancy had often noticed the family group around one of the larger tables in the dining room.

"She's nosy, too nosy for her own good," Bianca was saying, her eyes sparkling. "I know she is black and all, but that is not saying she a good person. She is not a good person. I don't like her and I stay away from people like that."

Interesting, thought Nancy. She knew Bianca was not a bigot. Nancy had seen her at dinner with other black residents, but Bianca had singled out Betts to dislike. What did Bianca know about Betts that would cause such bad feeling? Perhaps Jefferson's rudeness toward Betts was rooted in the same reason and was directed not at her color but her personality or some activity she engaged in. Nancy shrugged. Still, rude was rude, and, except for a tendency toward sarcasm, Nancy thought Betts friendly and pleasant and Nancy looked forward to meeting her again.

***

International Share Month

> In recognition of the national heritage of many of Whisperwood's residents, the display windows in the crafts rooms this month will feature the special arts and crafts our residents, staff, and their families brought with them from their native countries. Also in tribute to the multinational character of Whisperwood, the dining room menu this month will include entrees from countries all over the world. Celebrate our diversity!
>
> - *The Whisperwood Breeze, Newsletter for Whisperwood Retirement Village.*

CHAPTER 4

Nancy woke early the next morning. Malone usually slept on the bed, curled up next to her, but now he was fussing about something on the floor. She turned on the light and sat up to peer down at the cat, who had stretched out a tentative paw to bat a moving bit of black on the floor.

She pushed Malone aside to take a close look. A spider. A black spider. A black spider with a red spot on the back. Chills raced down her spine. She'd only seen one black widow spider in her life, and this one looked very much like it. Thank goodness Malone hadn't yet hit it with his paw or, worse, tried to eat it.

She reached over to her bedside table, picked up the water glass, drank the rest of the water, then upended the glass over the spider. She cajoled Malone into following her into the kitchen and gave him a treat. Then using the old trick of sliding a paper under the glass and spider, Nancy held the paper in place as she turned the glass over, shook the spider down into the glass and returned to the kitchen where she transferred the spider to a clean, wide-mouth salt shaker, adding a drop of water before closing the lid.

Maybe Louise can identify this guy for sure, Nancy thought, and suggest how it got into her apartment. Whisperwood's diligent cleaning staff were good at keeping bugs outside where they belonged. Could someone have slipped it under her door? She thought of the car racing toward her in the parking lot.

Later that morning, Nancy walked down the hall to the Whisperwood offices off the lobby in the central part of the building. Although the Whisperwood complex included other buildings, the main building comprised a central section of six stories that included the lobby, administrative offices, auditorium, beauty shop, dining room, and pub. Six-story wings extended out on the right and left to include the residents' apartments for independent living.

This was the day Nancy worked on *The Whisperwood Breeze*, the residents' newsletter. The lobby seemed quieter than usual, and the office of Harry Doyle, Whisperwood's administrator, was empty, which was odd. Ever since the fiasco last year when he had almost lost his job, he had come to work early, left late, and arrived promptly at meetings. She paused at the coffee station and poured herself a cup as Harry came through the front entrance along with the sheriff, a deputy, and the whiff of new-mown grass.

Harry was frowning, brows drawn together.

"What's going on?" Nancy asked.

He shook his head and hurried past her followed by the law officers. The sheriff tipped his hat to her, but the deputy walked on past as if he didn't see her. One of the benefits of age and a useful tool, Nancy thought, was to become invisible. Nancy walked over to the reception desk. "What's going on?" she repeated.

The young woman sitting there gazed blankly at Nancy with wide eyes and stuttered, "One of the residents was found dead this morning. In back by the woods. Shot." She shuddered. "She was shot! Here!"

Someone was shot at Whisperwood. Nancy's ears buzzed with the words. How could that happen in such a congenial environment? No wonder Harry was upset. "Who was it?"

The woman just shook her head. "I knew her. Been here a long time. Real nice lady. Odd name. Betts something."

Nancy stared at her. "Betts Horner?"

The receptionist referred to a note on her desk. "That's right. I'm waiting now for a call from her roommate."

Nancy felt sick. Betts Horner. Shot and killed. How could that happen here?

"And when the social worker comes in," the receptionist added, "she'll talk with the roommate and offer grief counseling. Then I get the name and follow up with whatever is necessary."

She picked up a sheaf of papers, but her hands were trembling. "That's what we do, you know." She tried a watery smile at Nancy. "When someone has died, I mean. We help the family with funeral and burial arrangements, disposal of the belongings, stuff like that."

Nancy nodded and turned away. She needed to sit down. Betts, that vibrant woman, was dead? There probably wouldn't be two women with that name at Whisperwood. Nancy sank into a lobby chair, her mind buzzing with questions.

Who would have shot Betts? Jefferson Lee Topham's rude behavior came to mind. His obnoxious attitude toward Betts was apparent to all, but would he actually pull a trigger? His bigotry wouldn't go that far, would it?

Then she remembered Bianca's unfriendly words. What was her problem with Betts? She couldn't imagine Bianca pulling a trigger at anyone either.

Did Betts have any other enemies? Were they actually enemies who bore her animosity because of who she was, that is, African American? An antagonism springing from the dark vat of racial hatred? Or something else? They might snub her, call her names, but shoot her at Whisperwood? Nancy shook her head in disbelief.

Betts had a roommate. Interesting. Was she—or he—just sharing the apartment or were they more involved?

Nancy had met Betts only once, but she had seemed like a pleasant, intelligent woman. Bianca was one person who thought otherwise. What was Betts really like? What kind of work had she done? Nancy could think of a number of careers that would generate the skills and knowledge that might threaten someone with a guilty secret. But did Betts threaten someone enough that he or she killed her?

Nancy thought of the attempt to run her down in the grocery store parking lot. Was there a connection?

The urge to act overcame her. She strode to Grace's apartment. Had Grace heard? Nancy stopped. She should wait until the family had been notified. And perhaps the news would be better coming from Whisperwood's social worker. Nancy turned around and walked back to the lobby. The social worker's office was behind the reception desk, and the door was closed.

"Has the social worker come in?" Nancy asked as the receptionist looked up. "May I see her?"

"I'm sorry, Ms. Dickenson. She did just come in with a client. You'll have to stay out here until she's available."

Nancy nodded and took a chair in the lobby. The receptionist was waiting for a call from Betts' roommate, so the social worker might be consoling one of Betts' friends, maybe Grace. Whoever it was would need a friend, and she could be a friend, even though she'd just met Betts and Grace.

Nancy took a seat in the lobby and waited to see who emerged.

Betts and Grace. How long had they known each other? None of her business, but Nancy always wondered about people and knowing more about each of them and their relationships enriched her experience with them.

She picked up a magazine and was leafing through the pages when she heard the double front doors automatically open. She looked over at the doors and saw her friend Louise stride into the lobby. Louise's thin frame was covered in an all-encompassing heavy white jumpsuit, and she carried a white pith helmet with veil and elbow-length, rubberized gloves. Her long, gray braid hung down outside the jumpsuit. She spied Nancy and waved.

"How are the bees?" Nancy asked.

"Buzzing along quite well, thank you." Louise ambled over to Nancy as she flicked her braid toward the crime scene van outside. "Who's that for? Usually they just bag them up and cart them away from the back of the building."

Suddenly Nancy choked up. Louise's words were too callous. They brought up memories of the friends she'd lost last year and the time she'd seen the bulky black bag on a gurney as she walked by an apartment. The image remained with her even though she had barely known the person. Nancy managed to spill out the name. "Betts Horner." She swallowed. "Betts was shot. I don't know anything more."

"Oh no." Louise sank into the chair next to Nancy's. She cast her eyes around the lobby as if seeking the culprit, then paused to stare at the social worker's office with its closed door. "Are we going through that again?" she asked. "I thought we got the bad guys out of here last year. Who's in there? Her roommate?."

"I don't know. Maybe Grace Maury, my neighbor. Just met them both yesterday and now. . ." Nancy took a tissue from her pocket and blew her nose. "They're trying to find the roommate. Did you know Betts?"

Louise sighed. "George and I sat with Betts, Grace and Grace's husband for dinner one night. You were taking a class and ate early. They were pleasant people. Enjoyed talking with them. I liked

Betts—she was feisty. Smart as a whip. My kind of person."

Nancy smiled and nodded. Louise was certainly that kind of person. She'd just won her campaign to plant native plants and remove the invasive species from the grounds of Whisperwood. What kind of fight would she get into now? Nancy thought of the tour brochure, but this wasn't the right time to talk about that. "Ever meet the roommate?" she asked.

Louise shook her head. "Seen her around. Betts said they'd been close friends before they tried living together. Lot of contention there."

"Must have been difficult." Betts said she'd lived at Whisperwood for three years. That was a long time to endure a bad living situation. "Why didn't one or the other buy the other one out?"

"Don't know." Louise shrugged.

"I'm waiting here to walk Grace back to her apartment," said Nancy. "That is, if she's the one in there. I don't know. Receptionist won't say."

"Confidentiality. I wouldn't want her to blab about me if I needed to see a counselor. No one else's business." Louise pursed her lips. "Grace's husband is probably out on the golf course, although he's out of town a lot." She tucked her gloves inside the helmet. "He travels a lot on business, they said, but looked to me like Grace is the one in charge."

"I haven't met him yet."

"You shouldn't wait here alone. I'll join you." Louise struggled with the zipper on her jumpsuit. "I'll just get out of this bee outfit and hide it behind the reception desk. I can pick it up later." She stepped out of the heavy suit that had covered her jeans and flannel shirt.

Louise was going to wait with her. The relief Nancy felt surprised her. She had been driven by compassion to find Grace and comfort her, even though Nancy didn't know Grace very well, but with Louise, with the two of them, this difficult time would be easier. For Nancy, anyway. She knew that she lived close to depression and this kind of thing could drive her deeper into the black hole. After her second husband's death, she had drifted too close to a suicidal melancholy. Thinking of Bill reminded her of the letter waiting for her in her apartment, and the thought upset her stomach. She pushed the letter out of her mind.

Thank goodness Louise had rescued her from those dark, lonely times by encouraging her to visit Whisperwood. Nancy's move to this retirement village of people, activities, friends, and good meals had saved her life. She refused to dwell on the murder and mayhem she had discovered at Whisperwood last year. She and the 90s Club had almost lost their lives then, but the important thing was that they had not. The culprits were captured or killed, and Whisperwood was back to being the safe and enjoyable home they expected.

Except that Betts had been shot. Killed. At Whisperwood.

The social worker's door opened. Grace, with red face and bleak eyes, one hand clutching a wad of tissue, emerged. Her black slacks and navy sweater fit the mood as if she already wore mourning. The social worker followed.

"Remember, I'm here whenever you need me," she was saying.

Grace looked down at her hands. "Thank you," she whispered.

Nancy and Louise stepped forward. "Hello, Grace," said Nancy. "We heard. We'll walk with you back to your place."

Grace managed a weak smile. "Thank you." She put her arm around Nancy's waist and leaned on Nancy as she walked. "Richard left this morning to go into town, you see . . . ."

"You can come stay with me," said Louise. "At least for tonight."

"Or with me," said Nancy.

She and Louise walked down the hall on each side of Grace.

"I can't believe it," Grace said. "Who would want to kill Betts?" She sighed and stared at the floor as they walked. "She was my friend. How can she be gone?"

Nancy's thoughts circled around the same questions. She patted Grace's arm as they walked.

"Come on down to my place for a cup of tea," said Nancy. "You too, Louise. It will help."

"All right. This is so sudden. . ." Grace dabbed at her eyes and blew her nose.

Nancy led Grace and Louise into her apartment, shooing Malone into the bedroom. He hurled a loud snarl at them as the door closed in his face.

Louise pushed a stack of magazines aside so Grace could sit on the sofa, but Grace shook her head. "Please. Back trouble. I'll just take one of the hard kitchen chairs."

Louise brought one in from the kitchen, then took another chair opposite the sofa as she used a tissue to dust off the coffee table. Nancy hurried into the kitchen and filled three cups with water, placed them in the microwave, put the sugar bowl on a tray, noticed the jar of pine pollen honey, added that, and returned to the living room. "It will just be a minute," she said.

"What can we do to help?" asked Louise, elbows on knees and looking at Grace.

Grace wiped her eyes with the tissue and gazed at Louise, then at Nancy with a grim set to her chin. "You can get whoever did this to Betts."

"Now you're talking," said Louise, with a glance at Nancy. "Nancy used to be a private eye."

Grace put down the tissue and managed a watery smile at Nancy. "I know. Everybody at Whisperwood knows that."

"Used to be. I'm retired now," said Nancy, getting up as the microwave buzzed. "Just a minute."

"Go on. I'll fill her in," said Louise, who proceeded to tell Grace about their adventures the year before and then, over the winter, in Fort Lauderdale. "We got the crooks, all of 'em, thanks to Nancy," she concluded.

"I didn't realize you'd done so much." Grace watched Nancy with something like respect in her eyes as Nancy brought out the cups and handed one to Louise and one to Grace. But as Nancy acknowledged the compliment, she saw something else creep across Grace's face. It seemed very much like calculation. What was she really thinking? Everyone had secrets and might not welcome a private detective. At the least, they would watch what they said, but maybe Grace simply had other mysterious heirlooms she'd like Nancy's help with.

"Whisperwood's Marketing Department keeps the bad stuff quiet," added Louise. "Better not to know for most people."

"Do you have any idea who might have wanted to hurt Betts?" asked Nancy.

"Jefferson, that scion of the old South, that's who." Grace spat out the words. "He plays the old Southern gentleman to the hilt, but he's a racist good ol' boy at heart."

Nancy nodded. Jefferson had seemed like a mean and bigoted old man, not above a hurtful jab at Betts. Was there something else going on between Jefferson and Betts? Was there a deeper meaning to the animosity? Did he have an alibi?

"What else can you tell us about him?" Nancy asked.

Grace wiped her eyes and looked at Nancy. "He worked for a tobacco company. . ."

"Scum of the earth," Louise grumbled, flicking her braid. "He sold his soul to the devil."

"Retired. He's descended from tobacco farmers." Grace shrugged. "His side of the family were always farmers. It's why they had slaves, but they lost the land years ago. His grandfather was the last farmer, but he wasn't much good at it. Jefferson's father managed someone else's land till it was sold to developers. Jefferson tried real estate for a while, didn't sell much, then he found a roosting place with a tobacco company."

Louise shook her head. "No moral sense at all. Tobacco companies are out to make money by killing people."

Grace looked at Louise and smiled. "Lot of money in tobacco."

"Is he married?" asked Nancy.

"His wife's name is Helen." Grace sighed and leaned back to stare bleakly at the ceiling. "You might call it a harmonious match. Couple of grown kids doing all right." She laughed. "They're not in prison anyway." She turned her head toward Nancy. "Sorry. I'm being nasty. Let's just say Helen shares Jefferson's opinions but handles them tactfully and with velvet gloves."

Nancy peered at Grace over her teacup. Grace looked tired and beaten. "I have a spare bedroom," Nancy said. "Why don't you go in there and take a nap. I'll put a note on your door that you're over here. That way, I can run interference so you won't have to talk to anyone you don't want to till you feel better."

"And if you really don't want to see anyone, you can hide out with me," said Louise, setting down her teacup and standing. "I'm up on the fourth floor."

"Thank you." Grace flashed each of them a weak smile. "I'd like to hide out for awhile. I still feel the shock." The smile turned grim. "And you're right. I don't want to see anybody else right now." She sighed heavily. "But I'll feel better in my own place. Richard will be home this evening. I'll be all right then."

"Meanwhile, we'll start looking for the bastard who killed her."

Louise said, arms folded and standing at the door like a sentry.

Grace smiled at Louise as she heaved herself out of the chair. "You do that."

***

Feeling Sad or Lonely?

Alice Adams and Whisperwood's team of qualified, experienced counselors are available 24 hours a day to help you cope with feelings of loneliness, loss, or depression. They are here to listen and help. Call them. Your visit will be completely confidential and private. They can help. Make an appointment today. 555-8900.

The Whisperwood Breeze, Newsletter for Whisperwood Retirement Village

CHAPTER 5

Nancy and Louise walked Grace back to her apartment and followed her inside. A robe had been tossed over a chair, and a strong onion smell drew Nancy toward the kitchen. The offending vegetable lay sliced on the counter along with two unbroken eggs and a green pepper. A skillet sat on an unlit burner.

It all looked quite homey to Nancy, who liked to see people, especially women, cooking good meals for themselves. In her opinion, cooking for one's self was a good thing. Before Whisperwood took over the cooking for her, she used to indulge in expensive gourmet items for meals.

Grace noticed the onion. "I was making myself an omelet when I heard. Sorry. So upset I forgot about it." She wrapped the onion in plastic wrap and placed it and the eggs in the refrigerator. "I'm sure not hungry now."

Someone knocked on the door. Nancy glanced at Grace, who whispered to Nancy, "I'm not here," and ran to the bedroom. Nancy stepped to the door and opened it.

A thin man wearing gray slacks, gray shirt, badge, and utility belt with holstered gun stood there. He looked as if he meant business.

"Hello, Sheriff Ambrose." Nancy put on a smile, but she remembered how patronizing he'd been. "I suppose you're here to ask Ms. Maury some questions?"

The last time Nancy had seen the sheriff was the previous summer when she and her friends in the 90s Club had almost lost their lives. He'd arrived too late for one culprit but in time to take the other one to the hospital. With grim humor, Louise had added two notches to her cane after that episode. Her wrist, broken in the fray, still gave her trouble. She'd added two more notches after their trip to Fort Lauderdale during the winter.

"Don't go, Nancy," said Grace, who had reappeared to hover near the bedroom door. "Or you either, Louise." She turned to the sheriff. "Please come in. I'm Grace Maury. I knew Betts, but not well, you understand? Have you made any progress?"

The sheriff doffed his hat and nodded at Grace, but he eyed Nancy suspiciously. Louise hesitated at the hall door, but Nancy threw her a warning look, took her arm, and unobtrusively pulled her into the living room, keeping a pleasant smile on her face. She didn't want to give the sheriff any reason to ask them to leave. The sheriff barely noticed them as he glanced around the apartment, frowning.

"May I get you some coffee?" Grace asked.

"No thank you, ma'am," the sheriff said. "I just need to ask you some questions."

"Take a seat, sheriff," said Grace as she sat on the couch, patting the place next to her for Nancy. Nancy would have preferred to stand where she was, but now she had to take the seat next to Grace. Louise sat on her other side. The three women gazed up at the sheriff, as if they were an audience waiting for his performance. Nancy regretted the arrangement. It seemed too confrontational and instead of being inconspicuous, they were the center of attention along with Grace. The sheriff sat stiffly down on the edge of a wicker chair with the red-flowered cushions. It creaked under his weight even though he wasn't heavy. He pulled a notebook and pencil out of a shirt pocket and set his hat down on the rug. "So you weren't close friends? People here tell me you spent a lot of time together."

"Not really," said Grace, "but I know who killed her, so you can stop looking right now."

The sheriff gazed passively at her, his eyes narrowed. The pencil in his hand hovered over the notepad. "Is that right," he said. "Now who would that be?"

Grace drew herself up. "My cousin. Jefferson Lee Topham. He moved here to rob me, and he hated Betts. You ask Nancy here." She sniffed. "There's no doubt about that. He did it, Sheriff."

The sheriff frowned at Nancy. "You agree with that?"

Nancy threw up her hands. "I don't know about hate. . ."

"I see." The sheriff wrote something down in his notebook before looking up to study Grace. "He lives here, does he?"

"For now," Grace said. "Third floor. He's the one you should be talking to." She lifted her chin and her eyes glinted in anger. "He's just here until he can wangle my antique clock from me. Then he'll find a reason to move, you mark my words. He'll reclaim his deposit for the Whisperwood apartment and go back to Richmond." She sat back with folded arms and glared at the sheriff.

The sheriff chewed on his pencil. "I thought you people were here for good until you, uh, passed on, I mean."

"We can change our minds," Nancy said quietly. "If some of us find we'd rather live someplace else, we can get our money back and move." She wouldn't, though. Her friends were here. She loved meeting them for meals in the pleasant dining room, taking the classes offered, going on the trips. She couldn't think of a better place to live. It was safe and secure, well, most of the time. Now that they'd gotten rid of the bad guys last year. Then she thought of Betts. Dead of a gunshot. Here at Whisperwood.

"Jefferson will," said Grace. "I guarantee it. Once he gets what he came for." Her jaw tightened as she looked at the sheriff. "You can't let him get away with killing Betts."

"I'll get the killer, ma'am." The sheriff leaned toward her. "Where might I find this Jefferson Topham?"

"Like I said, third floor, apartment 309. Back of the building." Grace shrugged, then added with a nasty twist, "Doesn't like the sun to fade his furniture."

The sheriff made a note. "Now, what can you tell me about the victim, I mean Ms. Horner. Did she have any enemies?"

"Of course not," Grace said. "She was a very nice person." Sometimes she had a chip on her shoulder, but you can't blame her for that. I moved in a few months ago, but she told me she's been here about three years. Time enough to make enemies, I guess, but not any who'd want to kill her. Why would they?"

Nancy thought of Bianca. How serious an enemy was she? Nancy glanced at her watch. Should be time enough to talk to Bianca before lunch and before the news had spread all over the building.

The sheriff looked up from his notes. "We're estimating the time of death as around one a.m. or early this morning, ma'am. Where were you at that time?"

Grace stared at him a moment. "An alibi? You think I need an alibi? I was at the concert in the auditorium last night. That's where. It didn't finish until ten, then I walked back to my apartment and went to bed like everyone else." She paused and glanced down at her hands. "With my husband. Ask him when he gets back from town. He'll tell you."

"I see." The sheriff wrote in his notebook. "What about you,

Ms. Dickenson? Were you also home in bed?"

Nancy remembered the concert. For once, she had decided not to go, preferring to finish the book she was reading. "In my apartment. Alone," she said, "and no alibi for one a.m."

"Me too," added Louise. "You'll be hard put to find anyone here who won't say they were home in bed that time of night. And a lot of us live alone. No alibis."

Nancy almost smiled at the confrontational tone. Louise was always ready to fight, even against the sheriff's legitimate questions.

"You could ask the insomniacs if they saw or heard anything," said Nancy to defuse Louise. "They sometimes meet late at night in the card room or library."

The sheriff made notes.

Grace went on. "If not Jefferson, then Betts must have been killed by some maniac out there, maybe somebody hunting in the woods who made a mistake. No one living here would do such a thing. Can't imagine what she was doing outside that late at night. She was a snoop, though. I knew that."

"A snoop?" asked the sheriff. "Why do you say that?" Nancy wanted to know too.

"She was nosy. Always asking questions." Grace shrugged. "Thought she'd never stop pestering me about that clock. Maybe she stuck her nose where it didn't belong."

"I'll find who shot her," the sheriff said and turned to Nancy with a slight smile. "You're pretty observant, Ms. Dickenson. What did you think about the, uh, victim?"

Nancy was still pondering Grace's description of Betts. It raised interesting questions, so she was surprised when the sheriff gave what sounded like a compliment along with the question. Sheriff Ambrose being friendly? What did he mean by it? Maybe she could open that door wider. He could be useful if he learned to listen.

And he was an elected official. He should listen. "I liked her, Sheriff, even if she did have a few rough edges. She was outspoken, though, and could have ruffled some feathers. Surely that wouldn't constitute a reason to kill her."

"You never know, ma'am. I've seen people killed because they frowned at someone and for all sorts of other flimsy reasons." He turned again to Grace. "I'd like a list of your friends and neighbors and anyone you've had dealings with here, ma'am. Do the same for Ms. Horner the best you can."

"I'll be happy to do what I can for you." Grace glanced at her computer. "I'll e-mail it."

"Soon as possible, ma'am." The sheriff picked up his hat and stood. "Is there anything else you can tell me?"

"If Jefferson didn't do it," said Grace, "maybe her roommate did. They didn't get along."

The sheriff frowned and wrote something down on his notepad. "Anyone else?"

Grace shook her head. She and Nancy walked him to the door. "Thank you, Sheriff," said Grace.

"Don't you worry about this, ma'am. We'll get the perp." He stepped out the door. "Ms. Dickenson, I'd like a word with you."

Uh oh, Nancy thought. Here comes the lecture. She put an arm around Grace. "Don't worry. Come over anytime. My spare room is still available if you'd like. We could get you settled there till your husband comes home."

"Don't bother, Nancy," said Grace. "I'll be fine here." She rendered a tentative smile.

Nancy nodded. "Come over if you change your mind. I'll be happy to have you stay with me." She followed the sheriff out.

They walked down the hall a short way, then the sheriff stopped and folded his arms. She was right about the lecture. Louise stepped behind Nancy, and the sheriff ignored her as he glared at Nancy.

"Ms. Dickenson, I know you're quite the detective. I've heard the stories, and I know what happened last year. But. . ." He looked her in the eye. "Don't go nosing around in this. There's a killer here, and it's likely he lives in this building. If so, he knows who you are and where you live. He's not going to like it if you get too close. He has a gun and he'll get you, too. I want you to stay out of this investigation, do you hear me?"

He put on his hat.

"Yes, sir, I hear you," said Nancy, smiling at the sheriff.

He extended his hand. "I expect your cooperation."

Nancy shook hands with him, and he turned and strode down the hall to the lobby.

Hearing didn't mean complying. If they hadn't interfered last year, there would no longer be a Whisperwood this year.

***

Special Deals Now on Spring Bouquets!

> Know someone who could use a colorful bit of cheer? Bonnie's Bouquets offers special rates on spring bouquets this weekend only. Free delivery to Whisperwood residents. Call 555-9100 today! Whisperwood resident receive an additional 10 percent discount.
>
> - *Ad in The Whisperwood Breeze.*

CHAPTER 6

Nancy walked back to her apartment with Louise, smiling to herself. Louise patted her on the back.

"The sheriff seemed wary but respectful," Louise said. "Not quite as patronizing as last year. We may have taught him a lesson. That and the voter drive. We're a thousand strong and can make an impact in the local elections."

"At least he sees me as a contender now and not just another sweet little ol' busybody here at Whisperwood." Nancy grinned at Louise. "A step forward. All good."

"All good," Louise repeated. "I'll head back to my place."

"Just a minute." Nancy pulled her door key out of her pocket. "I want to show you something."

Louise followed Nancy into the apartment. First Nancy picked up the jar containing the spider. Louise squinted at the half-inch arachnid at the bottom of the jar. She whistled and glanced at Nancy. "Where'd you find this?"

"In my bedroom. Malone woke me up sniffing at it." Nancy didn't like the look on Louise's face. "What is it?"

"Bad news. It's a black widow spider." She held the jar up to Nancy's face. "See the red hour glass on the back?"

"How on earth did that get into my apartment?:" Nancy glanced around at the clutter. "They're poisonous, aren't they?"

"You betcha," said Louise. "Maybe it wouldn't kill you, but you would be out of commission for awhile."

"Thank goodness Malone didn't eat it." Nancy watched the spider move around the bottom of the jar. "Gives me the creeps, but I hate to kill it."

"Let me take it," said Louise, putting the jar next to the door. "I'll release it out in the woods where it belongs."

"Thanks but be careful. Betts got shot somewhere behind the building."

"Late at night. This will be broad daylight with people around." She glanced at the jar. "Wonder how that critter got in here."

"I guess it could have hitchhiked on something brought in by a resident and then dropped off in the hall."

"Sure," said Louise, frowning.

Nancy picked up the tour brochure. "Take a look at this. You'll find it interesting."

"Don't try to sell me on that tour," Louise said. "Got too many things going on here."

"Read this." Nancy pointed out the offending statement. "They call it a 'tour for seniors' and limit it to people between fifty and seventy-five. Is that fair? Why would they do that? So arbitrary too."

Louise read the statement with disbelief. "That's ridiculous. I can see letting potential travelers know about hazards and difficult terrain or multiple steps that might pose problems, but to make an arbitrary rule like that?" Louise's eyes sparked. She pushed her lips in and out. "Age discrimination. I hate that kind of thing." She glanced over the rest of the brochure. "American company," she said, pointing out the address to Nancy. "We can get them." She grinned at Nancy. "All right. You've got me. I'll join you on this excursion. We'll show 'em and have some fun."

"And use our real ages," said Nancy.

"Yep. Let's sign up today. Right now." Louise looked at the computer. "Online. See what happens. If they give us any problems, I'll send them a list of people over ninety who run marathons and win canoe races."

Nancy felt like laughing as she sat down at the computer and turned it on. Louise was so predictable, still. . . "You're okay with this, aren't you?" Nancy asked. "I don't want you to think I manipulated you into the trip."

Louise shook her head. "I know what you did." She laughed. "I'm not a dummy, but someone has got to take these people to task. Both of us are ninety, we're in shape, and we can darn well do as well on the trip as one of their sixty-five-year-olds."

Nancy nodded. They found the website and filled in the form with credit card numbers to reserve the trip for later that summer. When Nancy tapped "Send," they looked at each other and grinned.

***

After Louise left, Nancy found Bianca's apartment number in the Whisperwood residents' address book and walked there, climbing the steps to the second floor over the pub. She crossed her fingers as she knocked on the door and hoped Bianca was in. A colorful square of cloth embroidered with a jungle scene, parrots, and Spanish words, hung from the door knocker.

Bianca answered the door, all smiles and eagerness. Her graying hair still showed black streaks, and she wore a colorful blouse out of Chico's catalog with a turquoise skirt and flip-flops. "Come in," she said with a dimpled smile, leading Nancy into the living room. "I am so pleased you visit me. Por favor, siéntese."

Nancy sat on a couch with red velvet cushions and arms of wood carved as a thick branch with leaves. A sturdy round wooden coffee table stood in front of it. Two armchairs on the other side of the coffee table matched the couch, but no rug covered the dark wooden flooring. With all the dark colors, the apartment would have felt shadowed and forbidding except for the open windows letting in the sunshine and warm breeze.

"I make you coffee, yes?" Bianca said, her eyes sparkling. "We visit, okay?"

"That would be nice," said Nancy.

"Okay, then." Bianca disappeared into the kitchen and reappeared almost immediately with two cups of coffee on a tray with silver cream and sugar pitchers. She handed a cup to Nancy. "Now. How are you?"

Nancy smiled. "I'm fine. How are you?"

"Muy bueno. Whisperwood is so very nice place." Bianca cast an eye around her apartment and smiled. "Muy bueno."

"We play bridge together," Nancy began, feeling her way along.

"Yes, yes. I know. Very fun game. I learn here, you know." Bianca clapped her hands.

"Last time we played together," Nancy took a sip of coffee, "you mentioned that you didn't like Betts Horner."

"Oh no. Was that bad?" Bianca clapped a hand to her mouth. "She is a friend of yours? I do not mean to hurt feelings." Her liquid brown eyes studied Nancy with concern.

"No, no," said Nancy. "I only met her once. But things have happened and. . .and I would like to know why you don't like her."

Bianca frowned. "I am a U.S. citizen. I have my papers and all in order. I have no problem with Immigration. They cannot bother me." She pointed to a framed document on the wall.

Nancy took a close look, noting the date, three years ago. Bianca's name in bold script was on the naturalization certificate.

"What would Betts have to do with your certificate?"

"You know she was with police. The government."

Of course. How obvious. Nancy almost smiled. Betts had worked in law enforcement with the government. That's what those ironic little comments Betts had made about Nancy as a detective were about.

An illegal alien wouldn't distinguish one law enforcement officer from another or with immigration officials. They were all government and the government could take everything. An illegal alien, even a legal one, even a naturalized citizen, might feel fear if they confronted any government agent, given the strong feelings against immigrants often quoted in the media. And Bianca knew Betts had been in law enforcement.

"Betts was retired, and police or government doesn't mean immigration necessarily," said Nancy. "And anyway, you were legally here in this country and a naturalized citizen."

"But she ask questions. Once I sit with her at dinner," Bianca said, her eyes tearing. "And she asked me where I was from, if I had other relatives here, what I did for a living. So many questions. Why does she ask questions? What is she looking for? She frighten me." Bianca pulled a tissue out of a box on the table and wiped her eyes. Then she looked at Nancy and lifted her chin. "And she knows she frighten me, but she no stop. She just smile and keep on and on. She upset me so much I can not eat my dessert."

"I'm so sorry. . ." Nancy began.

"But why you want to know this?" asked Bianca. "I have right to say what I think. This is America. She is bad woman." Bianca stopped and leaned toward Nancy. "Why do you ask questions about this bad lady?"

"I heard you talking about her at bridge," said Nancy. "It sounded as if you knew her and you didn't like her."

Bianca sniffed. "You are right."

"I didn't know her, but I had met her once." Nancy sipped the coffee to slow her pace and let Bianca catch up. "So I felt I needed to know more about what kind of person she was."

"Now you know, but I only one person. Other people might like her." Bianca shrugged. "You might like her too once you know her. You do not need my ideas." Her face brightened. "Ah, but you are private detective, not government. Maybe she could be big criminal, no?"

Nancy shook her head.

"So why do you want my. . .my opinion." Bianca said the word carefully as if unsure how to pronounce it.

"Because Betts has been killed by someone here."

Bianca gasped. "No! But me, I did not. . . I never. . . ."

"Of course not," Nancy said quickly. "No one suspects you. I just wanted to know a bit more about Betts, that's all. I don't think the sheriff will even question you."

"The sheriff!" Bianca fingered the blue glass beads around her neck. "I have nothing to say. Please, I do not want talk to sheriff."

Nancy reached over and patted her hand. "Don't worry. I won't say anything about you and probably no one else remembers or cares about how you felt about Betts. No reason to question you at all." After all, bringing in the immigration fears of someone who was an American citizen would only muddy the waters for the sheriff and might play into local prejudices.

***

Early that afternoon, Nancy walked down the hall, thinking about Bianca's fears. Had Betts been a bully as Bianca described her? Nancy stopped to select a wrapped piece of candy from a bowl on her neighbor's hall shelf as she passed. The apartment door opened. A stout woman with short, straight, steel-gray hair stepped out. She wore a brown pants suit. The jacket was open as if it were too tight to button, revealing a beige polyester blouse. .

"Nancy," she said. "Just the person I want to see. Could you step in a moment? I've got to talk to you."

"Of course, Elvira," Nancy said. She liked Elvira, a gracious and generous woman who was one of the few native West Virginians at Whisperwood.

"Have a seat. Coffee?" She glanced at her watch. "Perhaps a glass of wine?"

"Nothing, thanks," said Nancy, thinking that if she drank all the coffee or tea offered when she visited, she'd be awash.

Elvira stepped into the kitchen for a moment, then returned with a cup of coffee on a tray with cream and sugar and a plate of cookies. "Keep the coffee hot all day. Have a cookie." She sat down across from Nancy.

Elvira furnished her apartment in early American style with rocking chairs and a couch covered in a brown plaid pattern that matched the draperies. Nancy found the dull colors depressing and preferred tea to coffee, especially after Bianca's strong, dark brew, but she accepted a cookie.

"I have a problem," said Elvira. "Need to know what you think. You're the detective here." She sipped her coffee as she eyed Nancy with worried eyes. "I'm kinda scared."

Nancy hated to see a nice person like Elvira so upset. She leaned forward. "What's wrong?"

Elvira's laugh was hollow. "Apparently I'm in trouble with the IRS. I got a call from them last night. They say I owe back taxes and it's so overdue I need to wire them a check by the end of this week." She shuddered.

"Nancy, I don't have much, and I pay my taxes on time. I don't understand this. That man threatened me with prison." She gulped. "He scared me. I'm afraid. I don't want to go to prison."

"Did you send him any money?" Nancy held her breath.

"Not yet," Elvira stammered. "I don't have that much in my accounts here. I'll have to get it from my investments."

Nancy let out her breath. "Good." She reached across to take Elvira's hand. "This man who called you is a crook. It's a scam."

"What? But he knew all about me." Elvira looked at Nancy, doubt and relief in her voice.

"Yes, I think we'll have to explore that a bit," said Nancy, "but the IRS would not call you. No government agency would unless you called them first, and they needed to respond to your question. That goes for Social Security, Medicare, any of them. They would not call, and they would not threaten you like that."

"Are you sure?" Elvira asked. "They wouldn't call?"

Nancy shook her head. "So what exactly did he know about you?"

"He had my phone number. He knew I live at Whisperwood." Elvira reached for a tissue and wiped her eyes. "He even knew my bank—and my account number."

Nancy nodded and pressed her lips together. Scams like this were common and could originate anywhere in the world, except that he knew Elvira lived at Whisperwood. Everyone here used the bank that had a branch at Whisperwood. Easy to get the bank's routing number, then read it out to the victim as if he had the whole number and ask her to supply her account number to "identify herself." He called her so he had her phone number. That could have been random but knowing she lived at Whisperwood was not.

All Whisperwood residents used the same rural delivery address plus their apartment number. Whisperwood was not identified in the address or connected to a phone number.

Could Elvira's scammer be someone on staff? A resident? Someone in the area? How dare anyone frighten the people here.

Elvira tried to hide it but she was terrified.

"Don't worry," said Nancy. "It's a scam. Hang up the next time he calls. Intimidation like that is a well-known swindle attempt. If you really do owe any taxes, you'll get a letter, not a phone call. Guaranteed." And, Nancy wondered, how many other residents had been attacked like Elvira.

Nancy finished the cookie. "I'll bet something's going on here. I'm sure other people at Whisperwood have been contacted like that, too. You were smart to ask me about it." Nancy stood. "I'm going to put out a notice asking people to come forward if they've had threatening phone calls or e-mails. I don't think you're alone."

"I am so relieved." Elvira's smile was back and the sparkle. "What kind of people would do that?"

"Greedy people," Nancy said as she stepped out the door and walked on down the hall.

George met her in front of the pub. "You hear what Louise has got herself into now?" he asked.

As they all knew, Louise was always standing up for some cause or other, what the complacent called, "making trouble." Nancy shook her head with a smile. "Her bees attack somebody?"

"She tells me her bees are gentle, wouldn't attack unless they needed to protect their hive. Maybe I believe her, but I can't imagine anyone messing with a bee hive." George shuddered as he swung his cane to point toward the lobby.

Nancy turned and saw Louise sitting behind a table in the center of the lobby. No bee suit this time. She was back to wearing the beige vest with buttons. One large button that Nancy could read from a distance had the words "Pesticides" crossed through with a diagonal red line.

"Nancy!" Louise called, a grim smile on her face. "Come on down here. I need you to sign this." She waved a clipboard.

Nancy and George walked to Louise's table. Each of them took a clipboard from Louise. "Bees are essential for crops to produce the food we eat," said Louise in a loud monotone as if she'd repeated the words many times. "A pristine, monoculture lawn like we've got out there," Louise waved toward the outside doors, "is not. Sign the petition."

"What are you asking for?" asked Nancy, perusing the petition. So far, thirteen people had signed the one on her clipboard.

"I want the landscaping people here to quit using pesticides, that's what." Louise pushed a pen at her. "Sign."

Nancy signed. "I agree with this anyway, bees or no bees."

"Sure. We can go to a more natural way of maintaining the lawns. I like grass that's got a bit of diversity in it." Louise glanced out the front doors. "Diversity, that's what we need along with native plants." Louise was proud of her success the year before when she persuaded the Whisperwood Board of Directors to replace the exotic landscaping plants with native species.

"Mow higher, leave the clippings, bring in manure for the plant beds," added Nancy.

Louise grinned. "Mulch and rain gardens."

"All right." George hung his cane on his arm as he signed the petition. "Anything to keep you gals happy." He handed back the clipboard. "How many signatures you need?"

"A lot to convince the board to make a change." Louise glanced over the signatures. "The garden club is helping get signatures. Then we want to take over the landscaping management."

"The board pays some company to do that," said Nancy. "It's a big job."

"Excuse me." Louise squinted at Nancy. "I said management. We'd make the decisions on what to do and how to do it. The company would carry out our decisions. The ideas we have will make Whisperwood environmentally responsible and save the residents here a bundle."

"Sounds good," said Nancy. "Push that angle."

"Naturally," sniffed Louise.

"Say, Nancy. . ." broke in George, "have you heard anything about scams going on here?"

Nancy's ears perked up. "What have you heard?"

"Vera, my next door neighbor, you know her?" George leaned on his cane. "Saw her crying at the mailboxes. Hate running into that kind of thing. Damned awkward. Didn't know what to do, but had to ask if I could help." He cleared his throat and stared at the ceiling.

"What was wrong?" asked Nancy.

"Some mean-sounding thug called her. Said he was from a collection agency, said she owed $5,000 and better cough up. Wanted her bank account number, credit card number, stuff like that."

"Oh no." Nancy shook her head. Another one. "Did she give him that information?"

George pounded his cane on the lobby's tiled floor. "She did. He terrified her, pulled that information out of her, and he cleaned out her bank account. Used her credit card number, too."

"She call the sheriff?" asked Louise.

"I told her to," said George. "Nancy, maybe you could go talk to her. Tell her what's what."

"You'd think our people would be smarter than that." Louise straightened the clipboards on the table and eyed a woman just entering the front door. "I stopped responding to those kinds of calls—and e-mails—long time ago. Don't give out personal info to anyone."

"We need to plan a meeting to find out how many people have had those phone calls and to educate them about scams. Vera is just one of many, I think." Nancy glanced at her watch. "I've got to go. Good luck, Louise."

Louise nodded and turned away to approach the woman who'd just come in. Nancy knocked on Harry Doyle's office, heard a brusque "Come in," and opened the door.

Harry Doyle had been found innocent of any part in the unpleasantness the year before. With the strong recommendation of the 90s Club, the board had kept him on as administrator of Whisperwood. He had shed his business school suits and now wore a sweater over a casual shirt most days.

He put down a pen, pushed back his chair, and smiled up at her. "How is everything, Nancy? Not newsletter time again, is it?"

She shut the door behind her and sat down in the visitor's chair. "Not yet." The poor guy, she thought, as if he doesn't have enough to do just being administrator. She returned the smile. "I need to talk to you about a problem here."

Harry frowned. "I know. That poor woman. Betts Horner. Who would want to murder her?" His voice became stern. "But you are not to get involved. The sheriff has the investigation under control."

"I hope so," Nancy murmured. "But I'm talking about a different kind of problem."

"All right." Harry folded his hands on the desk, ready to listen. "What's going on?"

Nancy almost smiled at his earnestness. "I know of three residents who've been the victims of scams."

Harry arched an eyebrow. "Scams? Here? Nigerian princes with tons of money?" He shrugged. "Everyone gets those."

Nancy nodded. "Of course. This is more than that. We need to educate the residents on what is legitimate and what is not—and we need to find out who is targeting them." She explained how Vera had been victimized and made a mental note to tell Vera to contact the state's Consumer Protection Division.

Harry sat silently, pursing his lips as she spoke. When he didn't say anything, Nancy filled him in on the attempts to scam Maria and Elvira.

"There is one other thing." Nancy hesitated. "I hate to think this, but someone here might be the perpetrator. In Vera's case especially. Whoever it was knew the bank she used, a no-brainer if you knew she lived at Whisperwood, and how would you know that if you didn't know that her address was a Whisperwood one? Someone who lives here would be in an excellent position to know enough about a person's family and circumstances to fabricate a believable story for use in their scams."

Harry looked shocked. "But we do background checks on all resident and staff applicants. Our residents couldn't do something like that."

"Couldn't?" Nancy asked with a smile. "Yes, they could. We'd like to think they wouldn't, but people don't change their inclinations as they grow older."

Harry shook his head sadly. "I suppose that's true, but maybe if we get enough information from the victims or would-be victims, we could pinpoint who the crook might be—not that I believe anyone here would do such a thing."

"We should find out how many other people have been approached," Nancy added. "Has anyone talked to you?"

"No, they wouldn't. Maybe the social worker, I suppose." Harry mulled the problem, stroking his chin. "I'll call the West Virginia Attorney General's Office. They have a Consumer Protection Division. Ask them to put on a scam prevention program here."

"And if it's all right with you, I'll post a message on the bulletin boards, asking people to tell me of any attempts to extort money from them, either by the government, a collection agency, someone claiming to be a relative, or by any other means."

"Better make the social worker the contact person," said Harry. "People won't know they can trust you."

Nancy smiled. "I'll put down both of us. Some people might think the social worker constitutes big brother."

Harry laughed. "Gotta consider all angles in this business. I'll go talk to her now, tell her what's happening and ask her to work with you to prevent these scams."

Nancy stood. "I'll make some signs, and I'll be keeping my eyes and ears open."

Harry frowned at her. "I'm having second thoughts. The best way we can protect the people here is to educate them about scams and how to defend themselves. Don't go around and try to identify the perps yourself. You could get into trouble with the wrong person."

Nancy saw him hesitate. What happened to Betts was on both their minds. Did Betts find out who the scammer was? Was that why she was murdered? Or was she a threat because she had been in law enforcement? Nancy had another thought. *Was that why I was attacked in the parking lot?*

Nancy waved good-bye and left. Harry's was the second warning she'd received so far that day. She'd be careful, all right. She didn't want to be the second murder victim this week.

***

Rain Gardens Coming Soon!

Whisperwood's Garden Club will turn two low-lying spots on the grounds into water-using gardens featuring native plants. These rain gardens will absorb the rain and run-off from the grounds and keep the water from filling our streams with pollutants and debris. The use of native plants throughout the grounds, rain gardens, and other environment-saving initiatives are part of Whisperwood's new master plan. For more information, contact Louise Owens, 555-3566.

- *Garden Notes Column, The Whisperwood Breeze*

CHAPTER 7

With a bounce in her step and humming to herself, Nancy returned to her apartment, but as soon as she stepped through the door, she saw the pristine white envelope leaning against the lamp on her desk. It seemed to pulsate. Nancy could not take her eyes off it.

Standing in the doorway, she wished she could pulverize it. The shock had dissipated somewhat, but did she feel balanced enough to tackle the letter again?

She forced her eyes to move to the clock. Three in the afternoon. Plenty of time until dinner with her friends. Plenty of time to consider a response and get used to it. Deep inside, she knew the letter had already changed her life. What should her response say? What tact should she take? What would happen when she did answer the letter? Was she brave enough for that?

Nancy walked to the desk and picked up the envelope, hesitating before opening it. She, took a deep breath and reread the letter. What exactly was she to do?

During all the years of their marriage, Bill had never told her he had a child, a child born—Nancy hesitated at the old-fashioned phrase—out of wedlock while he had been married to his first wife, Nadine. He had had an affair, which meant, of course, that he had been unfaithful to Nadine. Nancy would never have thought that of

Bill, but now she had to reevaluate everything. Even her own relationship with Bill. She perused the letter again.

The child of that woman—Nancy felt like capitalizing the words—That Woman, had written the letter, exuberant, bold and unconsciously cruel. She wanted to meet with Nancy, her stepmother. How odd to be a stepmother at ninety. That Woman must have been much younger, very much younger, than Bill for her child to just now be in college. Nancy shook her head. Actually, the child must be a young woman, since she wrote that she was attending the University of West Virginia in Morgantown.

A thoughtless letter, really, its contents a bombshell. Her name was Ariana, and she knew her father, Bill as it turned out, had died before she could meet and really get to know him. She wanted to visit Nancy to find out what he was like.

Oh my. Nancy shook her head. How on earth was she to answer Ariana's questions when everything she thought she knew about Bill had just evaporated?

Had Bill ever cheated—she hated that word—on her? Their friends had thought them the perfect couple. Of course no one except the two people concerned could know what a relationship was really like, but she would have agreed with them until now. They were rarely apart even though he traveled frequently to gigs where he performed his magic act. When would he have found the time for another relationship?

Never. That was Nancy's response. They were too in love, too involved, too busy with each other to let someone else in. Which was one reason why, when he died, Nancy had spiraled into such a deep depression.

She looked down at the letter. She had to see this young woman, this Ariana. It was the right thing to do, and Nancy was curious about Bill's child, his daughter. But fear grabbed at her heart. Her image of Bill and their relationship was now irrevocably changed. What else would she learn when she met Ariana? The truth was, she was afraid, very afraid, to meet the girl who claimed to be her stepdaughter.

That evening, Nancy joined her friends as usual at table fifty-six in the dining room. She wasn't very hungry and ordered the vegetarian option, causing George to raise an eyebrow.

"Vegetarian, Nancy?" Louise said. "Are you feeling okay?"

Nancy managed a smile, but Ariana's letter had depressed her. "Just wanted to try something different tonight. That's all."

As she ate, Nancy gazed out at the many faces populating the dining room. Some of them were actively engaged in conversation, and Nancy could hear their occasional bursts of laughter. At a few tables, the residents focused on their plates rather than their table mates as they ate their way through the soup or salad, entree, and dessert courses which arrived in orderly but leisurely progression. Nancy's gaze stopped as her eyes met another's, a woman with such a bleak expression, such watery eyes over deep bags, such a quivering mouth that Nancy forgot her own troubles in the face of what seemed like deep tragedy or illness or both. She didn't know the woman, but she was going to find out who she was.

After dinner Louise walked with Nancy to her apartment. "I took care of the spider," Louise said. "It should be happy in its new home and not bother any of us ever again.

Nancy nodded, her mind elsewhere.

"Anything wrong?" Louise asked.

"What?" Nancy was so deep in her thoughts, wondering who that tragic-looking woman in the dining room was and what was wrong, that she had only absently realized Louise walked alongside. At least wondering about that woman had taken her thoughts away from her new "stepdaughter."

Nancy glanced at Louise. Was she that obvious? "No, nothing," she said. "Just not hungry, that's all. Except. . . ."

They had reached Nancy's apartment. Nancy heard Malone's scramble to the door and then his scratching at the protective metal plate covering the lower two feet of the door on the inside.

"Except what?" asked Louise, tapping on the door with her cane to tease the cat. They heard an impatient hiss followed by an angry meow from the other side of the door.

"Did you notice a woman two tables away who looked as if she'd seen her family die in a car wreck?"

Louise shuddered. "Whew. That's a vivid description. I think I would have noticed someone like that." She shook her head. "Didn't, though."

"She was sitting behind you. I can't help but wonder about her. She looked terrible." Nancy pulled her door key out of her pocket.

"Are you all right?" Louise asked. "You seemed abstracted and off your feed tonight."

Nancy forced a laugh. "I'm fine." She unlocked her door. "See you tomorrow."

"Okay. You know my phone number. Any time." Louise turned and hobbled back down the hall.

Nancy watched her. A slight misgiving surfaced. Louise was tough and active even if she did use a cane. She'd be fine on the cruise even if there were steps and rugged paths. At least Nancy hoped so. She gently opened the door. Malone jumped up and made a leap for the hall, but Nancy closed the door in his face. He looked up at Nancy reproachfully, yowled at her, then stalked with his tail high to his bed where he stared at her with narrowed, unpleased eyes. Plotting eyes, Nancy called them.

She didn't want to talk to anyone about the letter yet. She read it once more and then pushed it deep into the desk drawer. Phrases from the letter haunted her all night, creeping into her dreams and turning them into nightmares dominated by ticking clocks.

***

Amazing how a new day and a sunny morning can restore one's good spirits. Nancy felt much more optimistic the next day and met Louise, George, and Fitz in the pub for lunch. Tucked into a corner at the back of the lobby beside the dining room, the pub served sandwiches, soups, and salads but also stocked a full bar. It was a popular place for lunch or a pre-dinner cocktail.

Louise had come from the lobby and carried a tote bag of her petitions, pens and handouts. Jefferson Lee Topham and his wife Helen followed them in. Jefferson wore a dark gray suit with a pale blue shirt. A black string tie hung down from his collar. His wife was a bit heavy but still a fashion plate in white slacks, white angora sweater, and a gold chain necklace with matching gold earrings.

"May we join you?" Jefferson asked, the consummate Southern gentleman.

"Of course," said Nancy, ignoring George's raised eyebrow and Louise's frown. "Help us push a couple of tables together." She gave Louise a long meaningful look. Nancy wanted to know more about Jefferson, and she didn't want Louise's anti-tobacco activism to get in the way.

Louise nodded, but her face was grim. "We'll get it," said Louise, hanging her tote bag on a chair. She began pushing the tables together, using her good arm. She was still protective of the wrist fractured the year before. George woke up out of some daydream to help, but the job was done. Jefferson maneuvered his place next to Nancy.

"My wife, Helen," Jefferson said, with his arm around the woman on his other side. She dimpled a smile at them as she folded a napkin across her ample lap.

"I know you're from someplace in Virginia," said Nancy.

"'Deed so. Proud to be from the capital. Richmond." Jefferson had picked up the menu. "Y'all been here long?"

"A few years," rumbled George.

"Me too," added Louise, pasting on a smile and friendly attitude. She winked at Nancy. "Almost a year for Nancy."

"I'm a short-timer. Followed Nancy here." Fitz perused the wine list, then looked up to signal the server.

Nancy noticed Jefferson's frown at the inclusion of Fitz. Whisperwood had many African-American residents who, like everyone else, took advantage of all the amenities. Jefferson needed to open his eyes and his mind.

"What made you choose Whisperwood?" asked Nancy, looking at Jefferson. "I would have thought you'd stay near Richmond."

"I certainly wanted to," Helen said with a frown at her husband

"Now, dear. . . ." Jefferson patted her hand. "Grace and her husband Richard found this place. I'm afraid she always was a bit weak in family pride and station. I'm here to bring them around, get them to thinking straight. Family, you know."

Helen looked down at her plate and snickered as she muttered, "Thinking straight, now that's a good phrase." She smirked at Jefferson. "In fact, I kind of like it."

Nancy watched Jefferson place a hand on Helen's arm and squeeze. Helen yelped softly and threw him a daggered look.

But Nancy's mind was wrapped around Helen's comment. What did they mean by straight? Were they implying that Grace was a lesbian? Or a crook? Neither definition seemed to fit the Grace she'd met. Maybe it was just some private in-joke.

Jefferson smiled at the others around the table. "Grace has some family heirlooms that need to stay in the family."

"If she still has them," said Helen pointedly, coating her words with Southern syrup, "she gets to do what she wants with them." She reached over with a nasty smile and patted Jefferson's arm. "None of your business, sweetie pie. Time to let go."

Before Jefferson could respond, the server arrived for their orders. Nancy found Jefferson's comments intriguing. Family heirlooms. More than the clock, then. Valuable family heirlooms? Worth murdering for? Maybe. But then Grace wasn't murdered. Betts was. How could her death have any connection to Jefferson's family heirlooms?

"What kind of heirlooms," asked Nancy when the server had left. The history of such things fascinated her, especially if they were valuable enough to steal or cause family conflict.

Helen picked up her glass of iced tea. "A sterling silver bowl made by Paul Revere and engraved with George Washington's initials. Just for starters."

George rattled his teaspoon. "That's gotta be worth a fortune."

"Of course it is." Helen smiled at him as if he were a prize pupil. "But she has it, and we don't. I'm working on being real nice. Maybe she'll leave it to me in her will. Nobody else on her side of the family to take it unless her husband sees the money in it. No kids." She paused and Nancy saw her wink at George. "No close friends either, anymore, if you catch my drift."

"Helen!" Jefferson sounded shocked. "That's enough."

Nancy also felt shocked at Helen's words. No close friends left because of Betts' murder. Was that what she meant? What an odd and callous thing to say. Nancy picked up her glass of water as she stared at the centerpiece, a vase with a single daffodil, her mind assimilating Helen's words. So Grace and Richard had valuable heirlooms, and no heirs other than Jefferson and Helen. Could Betts have been such a good friend to Grace that she'd be in Grace's will? A possible motive for Jefferson or Helen to kill Betts,

Nancy supposed, but far-fetched. She assumed a bowl by Paul Revere engraved with George Washington's initials might be worth quite a lot, but enough to kill for it? If so, did Grace have it here at Whisperwood? Was it in a safe place? Would Grace be the next victim if the bowl was so desirable? Nancy's mind came back to the group, and she realized Jefferson was talking.

"We moved here to get closer to them, cement family relations, you know," Jefferson smiled at them. "Imagine our surprise when we found she'd taken up with that. . .that person."

Could he actually mean Betts? Was he talking about her race or something else? Nancy glanced at Helen for her reaction, but Helen's attention was diverted to searching the room for their server. She spotted him and snapped her fingers, holding up her iced tea glass.

"Refill," she said as she patted Jefferson's arm and turned back to talk to them. "Of course, we feel the heirlooms should remain in the family. My daughter has a fine colonial home in Richmond where they could be displayed appropriately for everyone's enjoyment. The heirlooms could be passed down to her children and remain in the family."

"Grace has them in storage," Jefferson added with a frown of distaste. Behind him, a server carried a tray heavy with plates and glasses. "Hidden away. Doesn't show them. Doesn't use them. I don't even think Richard knows where they are."

"No good to anyone." Helen leaned forward, "She is just selfish. That's why her other two marriages didn't last. At least one of them had life insurance. Not much but she got it when he died." Helen tittered. "Or she killed him."

"That's enough, Helen," Jefferson said.

But Helen rattled on. "We don't even know if either Grace or Richard has a will. Anything could happen to that stuff when they're gone. Jefferson has talked and talked to them about it, but Richard's used to deferring to Grace and Grace hates us."

"Now, now, my dear." Jefferson looked meaningfully at Nancy. "I'm only interested in the old clock, which has many sentimental memories for me."

"Really?" Nancy said. "Why is that?" Perhaps there would be a clue here to the puzzle.

Jefferson laughed. "Have you seen it? Too ornate for modern tastes. Of no interest to anyone whatsoever, but my daddy used to keep it on his desk and I used to play with it. Put it in the shop window now and then. Memories, you know."

Nancy caught the slight smile that crossed Helen's face and wondered what it meant. She didn't think Jefferson had fond memories of the clock, but he seemed to think he could sell this idea to them. What would Grace say?

Fitz stirred restlessly and tapped his fork on the tablecloth. "I'm concerned about what's going to happen with the sheriff's investigation of Betts' murder. Have you talked to him, Nancy?"

Nancy waited until the server had set their plates down and withdrawn. "I have met him, and he's proceeding with strict instructions that we are not to interfere."

"But of course not," Helen said. "That's his job."

Louise, George, and Fitz exchanged glances. Nancy picked up her sandwich. "We don't want him to go astray," she said. "He doesn't know the people or the situation here."

"Yeah," Louise broke in. "He's liable to collar anybody who looks possible. And right now," she peered across the table at Jefferson, "seems to me that's you."

"Me?" Jefferson had picked up his sandwich and stopped with it halfway to his mouth. "I don't know anything about it. Hardly knew the woman."

"Of course not," Helen said. "We've just been here a short while so Jefferson could get to know his cousin. Of course we were appalled to hear about the life she leads here." She glanced at Jefferson. "And that. . .that person. Grace was brought up in a decent southern family. We are ashamed of her. We truly are."

What were they saying? Was Betts then more than just a friend? Nancy bit into her sandwich as she watched Jefferson nod his head. The venom in Helen's voice was palpable. Were they here to "change" Grace? Make her conform to their expectations of southern womanhood? Jefferson had chosen an expensive way to do it, but perhaps Helen was setting up a smoke screen and their motives were different. What was she hinting at? It must have something to do with the old clock, in which he seemed to have a special interest. She studied Jefferson, the epitome of a southern gentleman. A bigoted southern gentleman. He and his wife had no kind words to say about Grace or Betts.

"I like Grace," said Louise in a firm voice. "And I liked Betts. She was a good person. She not only signed my petition but offered to help."

"What petition?" asked Fitz in his Jamaican lilt. "What kind of rabble-rousing are you into now?" He winked at Nancy.

Louise reached into her tote bag and pulled out a sheet of paper and a pen. "Here. Sign. We've got to change the way we do the landscaping here. It's killing the bees."

"Bees!" shrieked Helen. "I don't want bees coming around me."

"Bees won't bother you," said Louise. "Unless you mess with their hive. They might be interested if you're wearing stinky perfume. Just leave it off when you're wandering around outside on the property, that's all. Ought to leave it off outside anyway. Bees aren't going to sting you unless you do something obnoxious to them."

"I'm certainly not signing that petition," Helen sniffed.

Louise frowned at her a moment, then shrugged and turned to Nancy. "We've got another problem here. What are we going to do about the scams hitting the residents all over the place?"

Nancy nodded. "I've talked with Harry about that. Probably too hard to find the scammers, but we can arm the residents. We're working on putting together a seminar on scams and frauds to help the residents guard against them."

"Good, but those scams can be devious and convincing," said Louise.

George thumped his cane. "Speak up, will ya? You mean Vera's not the only one?"

"What's that you say?" asked Fitz.

"George and I have been using computers for a long time," began Nancy. "We're used to deleting the million dollar offers from Nigeria, and we're wary of the fake websites and the other sneaky ways con artists use the Internet."

Louise nodded. "But there are a lot of newbies at Whisperwood whose kids gave them a computer or an I-Pad, and they've taken the computer classes here, so now they're feeling real proud to be on the Internet. They don't know yet all the devious tricks con artists use to get personal information."

"You don't have to be a newbie on the computer," said Nancy. "Some of those scams are so clever, I've almost been taken in. Stopped just short of giving out a credit card number to a dubious site once. Phone calls, too." Nancy bit into her sandwich and chewed thoughtfully. She swallowed and added, "Maria Schmidt got one of those calls supposedly from her grandson."

Louise groaned. "I've gotten that one too. Told 'em where to go. I agree with whoever said hanging up ain't rude, it's shrewd."

George laughed. "That's my Louise, all right."

Louise glared at George, then turned to the others. "I heard that

Harry contacted the Attorney General's Office. They're going to send someone from the Consumer Protection Division down here to speak to all of us."

"Excellent, Luv," said Fitz, smiling at Louise. But, I say, it's a bit much the way the scammers go after us seniors."

Louise nodded. "I know. The crooks target us because they think we have a lot of assets, have trouble remembering things, and we're so lonely and isolated, we'll talk to anybody who calls us, even strangers."

"Ha!" George interrupted. "I hide in my apartment just to get a minute alone."

"That's because you live here," put in Nancy, "and not independently in your own home, alone and lonely."

"Over-rated, if you ask me," said Louise. "We also value courtesy. They trade on that and also that we're not likely to report it when we've been scammed."

Jefferson and Helen sat back, watched, and said nothing.

But Nancy was worried. Louise was right. This place was full of potential victims. She had not received a threatening phone call but others had. The caller seemed to know specific information about his victims. Easy information to get if you lived at Whisperwood and contributed to the residents' biographical directory, available for all to read in the fifth floor library. Nancy had removed the page about herself. She'd been a detective too long to want personal information bandied about.

Even so, it was well known at Whisperwood that she had been a private detective. Was that why she had not received any of those scamming calls? She hated to think what that meant.

***

Later that afternoon, Nancy climbed to the fifth floor for a visit to the library, thankful that with video cameras installed in the stairwells, the stairs no longer posed the menace they had in the past. Thinking of the residents' directory reminded her that the biographies also often included a photo of the resident. The tragic mien of the woman she'd seen in the dining room haunted her. Who was she and what was wrong?

Nancy sat at the library table, the three volumes of the directory in front of her. She leafed through them quickly and scanned the biographies for Maria, Vera, and Elvira, seeking any kind of common denominator. Aside from being women and living alone at Whisperwood, there didn't seem to be any. Then she leafed through the first volume but found no entry with a photo that resembled the tragic woman. Towards the end of the second directory, she found the woman at last in the "P" section.

Alicia Perrygrew. She had moved in six years before with her husband who died several months later. She had a son who lived in Wyoming and a daughter in Connecticut. She had worked as a preschool teacher after her children started school. Her husband had owned a convenience store in Fairfax, Virginia. They had retired and traveled and as they approached eighty years old, they had moved to Whisperwood. Alicia liked long walks and reading.

Nancy noted Alicia's apartment number and closed the directory. Nothing there to indicate any deep tragedy. Had she been diagnosed with some disease? Had something happened to her children or grandchildren? How could Nancy meet her and strike up a conversation? Alicia did not frequent any of the usual meeting places or Nancy would have seen her before. She did not belong to the bridge or garden club, and Nancy had not seen her in the gym or the pool. What did she do here? The biography did note that she liked to take long walks and to read. Nancy resolved to improve her exercise regime by increasing her walks around Whisperwood.

***

Celebrate West Virginia Day
And Family Fun
June 20

Whisperwood invites residents to bring their families here for our annual Family Fun Day on Saturday, June 20, the day West Virginia became a state. The pond will be stocked with fish and fishing rods provided for the fishing tournament, the pool will be open, and hot dogs, hamburgers and all the fixings will be available at picnic tables on the grounds.

Please let the receptionist know how many in your family will attend by Saturday, June 13, so we'll have enough food for everyone.

- *The Whisperwood Breeze, Newsletter for Whisperwood Retirement Village*

CHAPTER 8

After dinner that evening, Nancy cleaned out Malone's litter box as she thought about the puzzle of the old clock. What could its secret possibly be? She finished the task and then carried the large and bulky clock to the dining room table. Even considering its family history, why would Jefferson be so interested in such a feminine piece with its flowers and furbelows?

She took out a notebook, drew a quick sketch of the clock, and then began to write down a description to use in case Grace asked for the clock back. Grace might decide to give up trying to solve the puzzle, but Nancy intended to find the answer or confirm that the clock was simply that, a clock.

The case was made of porcelain, Nancy wrote, and it was covered with delicately sculpted flowers. The porcelain base was separate. She retrieved a tape measure from the desk drawer. When the clock was placed on the base, the whole piece was seventeen inches high, eleven and a half inches wide and nine inches deep. The clock face was white, but the roman numerals were engraved in black. The filigreed hands were also black.

Nancy searched the Internet for a similar clock and found its exact match for auction on eBay.com. It was described as an ornate mantel clock made in Paris, France, circa 1840 to 1860, by Henri

Marc. Before America's Civil War then. An additional note called it an eight-day clock with spring wound movement and a bell that struck on the hour and half hour. Nancy checked the e-Bay auction site and found the high bid so far was fifteen hundred dollars with twelve hours remaining.

She ran her fingers over the outside as she studied the antique clock. It was still ticking from when Grace had wound it up. The time was not quite correct. After all these years, the mechanism needed adjustment. She opened the back. Perhaps there was some message tucked inside. Or a map. Maybe a vial of diamonds? Nancy's imagination took flight with the possibilities but fell flat when she found nothing but the clock works and the winding key. Her fingers explored farther into the body of the clock. Still nothing. No message, map, or diamonds taped to the inside.

She examined the casing but discovered no hidden recesses and no secret compartments. The numbers were simple Roman numerals. The dots representing the minutes around the clock were evenly spaced and sized, so they weren't Morse code or a binary code or some other kind of code or cipher. The dots weren't microfilm either. Nancy tried to scrape them off gently with her fingernail, but all were engraved into the clock face rather than attached. Hard to hide microfilm in, on, or under the dots or the numbers.

She removed the hands so she could detach the face of the clock. She found only the clock works. Nothing out of the ordinary.

Nancy sat back and studied the clock. She'd tried all the obvious possibilities. Perhaps it wasn't the physical clock itself but what it stood for to Jefferson. Another reason to talk to Grace.

She knew a bit more about the clock but had discovered nothing to indicate a puzzle or any kind of mystery. She took the clock back to her bedroom and returned the tape measure to the desk drawer. As she opened the drawer, she thought of the letter hidden inside. She was afraid there was little mystery there, but she needed more time to adjust her thoughts and consider how to respond. What was she to do about the unexpected dilemma posed by her new stepdaughter Ariana?

Nancy immediately derailed her thoughts onto the mystery of Alicia Perrygrew. When did Alicia take her long walks? How could Nancy find out? Could she invent an excuse to visit Alicia at home in her apartment? Nancy had no doubt that Alicia was deeply troubled and needed help.

***

Sign Up Now for Computer Genealogy Class

Back by popular demand! Whisperwood's well-known genealogist Agnes Wilson has agreed to repeat her popular class on using computer databases to help residents track their family back through the generations. Space is limited, so sign up now. Registration forms are available at the central reception desk. Fee for the class is $15 plus an additional $25 for materials. Any questions, contact Agnes Wilson at 555-3028.

- The Whisperwood Breeze, Newsletter for Whisperwood Retirement Village

CHAPTER 9

Despite the horrifying experience in the grocery store parking lot on her last visit to town, Nancy planned a trip back to town early the next morning. She wanted to get away from Whisperwood and her troubling thoughts for a couple of hours. A drive would be just the thing.

She made a quick call to Louise.

"Sure, I'll go with you," Louise said. "I need to pick up a few supplies at the farm store. Meet you out front in fifteen minutes."

Right on time, Louise stepped out of the elevator and waved at Nancy in the lobby. This time, Louise wore a "Don't Litter" button on her vest. Nancy slowed her pace to match Louise's hobble as they walked to the parking lot.

Halfway there, Louise held out an arm to stop Nancy. "Just a minute," she said. She stepped off the sidewalk onto the wet grass and peered down at something near her feet. Nancy admired the sparkling dew drops on grass and shrubbery as she waited for Louise to inspect the tiny spring flowers hiding in the grass.

"Just checking." Louise returned to the sidewalk, brushing her hands. "Hope they've kept the pesticides off."

"Me too," said Nancy. "I'm glad you're keeping a watch on what they're doing here."

Louise paused and shielding her eyes from the sun, surveyed the parked cars. "I used to have a pick-up. Handy. Sure wish I hadn't given it up when I moved here."

"I'll drive you wherever you want to go," Nancy said. "Anytime. I like to drive." She gazed affectionately at her Prius' silver sheen. To herself, she always called every car she'd owned a roadster, just like her first car so many years ago. The adventures they'd had!

She backed the car out of the space and drove through the gate, waving to the security guard in the gatehouse and the two Rottweilers, Ham and Eggs, still in their pens behind the gatehouse. Nancy began to feel freer and smiled at Louise who grinned back at her.

They had gone only about a half mile down the two-lane mountain road when Louise yelled. "Hey, stop, Nancy!"

Nancy pulled over. She had to press down hard on the brake to roll the car to a stop. "What?"

Louise had already stepped out of the car and walked back to a pile of trash alongside the road. "Look at this," she said in disgust. "What kind of boneheads have to mess up a beautiful spot like this?" She waved at the trees, bursting out in new spring growth, on both sides of the road. She put her hands on her hips. Her eyes sparked with anger.

"I just can't believe some people," she muttered. She pulled a plastic garbage bag out of her vest pocket and used a stick to pick up the trash and put it in her bag.

She glanced at Nancy. "Sorry. Can't let this stay here. Turtles could die feeding on the plastic." She picked up a six-pack holder of plastic rings. "A critter could strangle in this."

Nancy leaned against the trunk of her car. "Go right ahead. Glad you're doing it. Wish I'd thought to carry bags to pick up trash." She didn't hear any cars coming up the mountain, only the hum of insects and the sweetness of bird songs. Nancy took a deep breath and let it out slowly, feeling the serenity of green trees, blue skies, warm breezes, and the cloying scent of early honeysuckle.

Louise stood and twisted the neck of the bag shut. "Okay. Much better now."

Nancy nodded. "Yes, much better now." But as she pushed herself off the car, she glanced up the road behind them, then looked closer. A line of something wet trailed behind her car. She reached down and dipped her finger into the reddish stream of fluid. She squinted at the smear on her finger, then she sniffed it. Brake fluid.

She walked to the front of her car. No trail extended forward. The fluid must come from her car. She'd had enough experience with malfunctioning cars and car maintenance to know brake fluid. She sniffed it again to make sure. Her car was leaking brake fluid. That explained the slow stop when she pulled over. She shaded her eyes to look down the mountain. They had at least a mile to go down the curving mountain road until it evened out in the valley.

"What's wrong?" asked Louise, putting the bundle of trash in the car trunk.

"Look at this." Nancy held out her finger with the reddish smear for Louise's inspection, then pointed to the fluid trail leading back up the mountain toward Whisperwood.

Neither one spoke for a moment.

"When did you last have your car serviced?" asked Louise. "Is this something that happens a lot?"

"Serviced just a month ago," Nancy opened the hood and peered at the brake fluid container. It was almost empty, but she couldn't check under it to look for a leak or loose connection.

"Could someone have cut your brake line or whatever it is they do to cause a leak?" asked Louise, hands on her hips.

"Maybe." Nancy said, pulling a tissue out of her pocket to wipe off the smear. "Someone almost killed me at the grocery. But why?"

Louise pursed her lips. "Let me guess. Famous detective and a murder at Whisperwood. Hmmm." She looked at Nancy. "Third miss. Time to pay attention."

"Three misses?" Nancy asked.

"One, attempted rundown at the grocery store. Two, black widow spider in your bedroom. Three, leaking brake fluid. Can I make it plainer than that?"

"But the grocery store near-miss was before Betts was murdered. I wasn't involved in anything that would concern anybody."

Louise shook her head. "But you are involved in a murder now. That's got to worry someone."

Nancy walked to the driver's side and slid onto the seat. She needed to sit down and pull herself together. Leaking brake fluid. They could have been killed. She shivered just thinking about what might have happened.

Louise was right. That near-miss in the parking lot was no accident. Then the black widow spider. Could it really have found its way into her apartment from the outside? How? The only stuff she brought into the apartment was practically sanitized groceries from the supermarket. Nothing a spider could hitchhike on.

The custodial staff were diligent at keeping the hallways and doorways clean, and no clutter was allowed in the halls. Someone must have released it in her apartment. Under her door? Through a window? Could a visitor have done that?

And now this leak in her brake line. Who wanted her dead? Why? She knew nothing about Betts' murder. She looked at Louise. "I'll have the garage check the line."

"Good. I'll call for a tow truck and a ride back to Whisperwood," said Louise as she pulled out her cell phone.

***

Al's Garage Offers Special Rates to Whisperwood Residents

Schedule your regular car maintenance at Al's Garage. Oil change with new filter, tire checks, balancing and rotation, and all other service needs will be handled efficiently and quickly. Special low rates for Whisperwood residents. We'll beat all other offers in town. Al's Garage is conveniently located on Main Street one block from the Food Lion.

- Ad in The Whisperwood Breeze, Newsletter of Whisperwood Retirement Village

CHAPTER 10

Nancy made the rounds greeting the residents at other tables in the dining room that evening, looking for any hint of surprise at seeing her alive and well, but she was greeted as usual. No one seemed at all disappointed, upset, surprised, or annoyed at her appearance. As she took her regular seat at table fifty-six, she concluded that someone at Whisperwood was either an excellent actor or didn't know she'd taken her car out.

George sat fuming as he heard Louise and Nancy describe the incident. Fitz rubbed his chin back and forth. "You're sure the line was cut?" he asked.

"The mechanic called Nancy and confirmed it." Louise's eyes sparked. "Said we wouldn't have made it to town alive."

Nancy tapped the table with nervous fingers. "He's reporting it to the sheriff who will find a way to blame me. He'll insist it was all my fault for interfering with the investigation. I can hear him now."

"You wouldn't have to interfere if he would do his job," added Louise. "The important thing is that we have to watch out. All of us." She looked at Nancy. "You especially, Nancy. I don't think they were after me."

"Anyway, it was Nancy's car," said Fitz. "Third go at trying to get rid of you, right?" He put his hand over Nancy's. "We need to find the culprit fast. Get him before he gets Nancy."

"But exactly why does he want to get rid of Nancy?" asked Louise. "What is he afraid of?"

Fitz sat up and cast a glance around the table. "Nancy's reputation as a detective is fearsome. We've had a murder and we're besieged by scam attempts. Of course they're afraid of her."

Nancy held up her hand. "Apparently just walking around makes me dangerous to someone, and I'm not going to stop that. I'll just take extra care around here and put off any trips to town. If I don't feel safe, I'll stay with Louise till this is over."

"Welcome anytime." Louise lifted her water glass in a salute.

The next morning, Nancy dressed in khaki slacks and black turtleneck and combed her curly hair, glad that it was short and easy to manage. She fed Malone and gave him extra pets, then took a book to the lobby to read while Louise badgered passersby to sign her petition. Everyone at Whisperwood, newcomers and long timers alike, had heard how Nancy and the 90s Club had saved Whisperwood the summer before. Most were willing to sign the petition in gratitude. Many were as concerned as Louise about the devastating loss of honeybees worldwide.

Nancy looked up as Helen sat down beside her, waving her coffee cup in Louise's direction. "Quite the little social activist, isn't she?" Helen sneered.

Nancy ignored the sarcasm. "Louise does important work, and she's right. We should all support her."

"Not me. Bees sting and anyway they're bugs." Helen turned toward Nancy and whispered. "I heard Grace's little friend was picked up by the medical examiner. Everyone is saying she was murdered, which I find hard to believe."

Nancy stared at Helen. "You must know that Betts was shot.

She certainly didn't shoot herself."

"Must have been an accident." She laughed. "I mean, here? At Whisperwood? Ridiculous." Helen's voice dripped with malice. "Anyway, most of Grace's friends come to a bad end, you know."

Nancy smothered a gasp of surprise. "What do you mean, her friends come to a bad end?"

Helen studied her fingernails and shrugged. "She doesn't keep friends long," Helen smiled, "although they usually leave while they're still alive." She looked at Nancy with an arched eyebrow. "We've always known Grace was a bit cuckoo." Helen tapped her head. "We don't trust her. You shouldn't either."

Before Nancy could come up with a response, Helen rose, twiddled her fingers at Nancy, and walked down the hall.

Nancy kept her face blank but she was appalled at the venom in Helen's comments. Nancy knew people who might say that she didn't keep friends long either, since both her husbands had died, one at a fairly young age, but both of natural causes. Of course, Louise was still a friend. They'd known each other since school days. Grace probably had long-time friends too. They just didn't happen to live here.

What was Helen trying to do? Solve Jefferson's problem and Betts' murder through gossip? Were they trying to pin the murder on Grace? That might be one way to get hold of the clock, but was it worth that much?

Had Helen spread this bit of nonsense to Sheriff Ambrose? What was she saying about others here? Nancy's eyes narrowed. *Or for that matter, what is she saying about me?*

***

After lunch, Nancy knocked on Grace's door, hoping Grace would be up and willing to talk about the clock and perhaps even about Betts. The door opened a crack and an eye peered out.

"Just a minute, Nancy." The door closed.

Nancy waited, then she heard the chain drop. The door opened wide enough for Grace to reach out and pull Nancy in.

"I'm so glad to see you," Grace said. "People have dropped by, but I haven't opened the door to anyone. Afraid the sheriff would be back, and I'm just not up to answering his questions. "I don't know anything."

"Of course not," said Nancy, full of sympathy. "How could you know anything? Are you all right?"

"I'm over the shock of it." Grace pulled her fleecy pink robe closer around her body. "Richard helped me get through the night." She saw Nancy glance at the bedroom. "He's not here. Golfing with his buddies." She sighed. "I'll miss Betts. It was just horrible." She sat on the flaming red couch. The pink robe seemed to tame it. "Take a seat, Nancy. Would you like some tea?"

Nancy sat in the cushioned wicker chair and shook her head. "No thanks. I won't be long." Grace seemed more relaxed now. She wasn't surprised, more like pleased, to see Nancy, which went a long way toward eliminating her as a suspect in cutting the brake line. Not that Nancy actually suspected Grace, but suspicion was a habit. There was no reason for Grace to want to get rid of her. Nancy put these thoughts aside and got to the real subject of her visit.

"Would you feel like talking about the old clock?"

Grace sat up, surprised. "I've been so upset, I forgot about it."

"I have been working on it," Nancy said.

"Found out anything yet?" Grace leaned toward Nancy, interest written on her face.

Nancy shook her head. "Did that clock have any sentimental meaning for Jefferson?"

"Of course not." Grace snorted. "Ridiculous. Whatever that clock means for Jefferson, it's represented by cold, hard cash. That's all. I just want to know what there is in the clock that makes him think there's money in it."

Nancy heard the faint sound of a phone ring. Grace fumbled with her robe and slipped her feet into a pair of pink mules. "Excuse me. I have to get that." She hesitated. "Still trying to reach Betts' friends." She withdrew into the spare bedroom and closed the door. Nancy got up and walked over to the double glass doors leading out to the terrace. A lone lawn chair stood on the terrace but no potted plants. Nancy glanced at the fake ficus in the living room and thought of the plastic flowers on Grace's hall shelf. Obviously, Grace did not have a green thumb. Nancy walked back to the chair. She heard the loud drone of the mowers outside. Had Louise gotten them to increase the mowing height yet?

After a few minutes, Grace returned. "Sorry about that. Just some business. Have you come up with any ideas?"

"I didn't realize this was a two-bedroom unit," said Nancy, "like mine, only a bit larger, I'd say. And you have a terrace."

"I decided on Whisperwood's largest unit. Richard and I both need our space, you see."

"Of course." Nancy could use more space too, living with Malone. So could he. "About the clock. I can't find anything inside or outside that looks like it might be connected to a secret."

"Betts and I couldn't either. I can't imagine why Jefferson wants it so much."

"It does look like a collectible," Nancy said. "I found one like it on the Internet that could go for more than fifteen hundred dollars."

"Jefferson doesn't collect anything," Grace sniffed, "except real estate and civil war weapons and memorabilia. Southern style. I'm sure that clock doesn't qualify, and it's so fancy. A bit over the top, if you ask me. He'd sell it immediately." She paused to sniff. "Unless there is a secret to it that's worth more."

"It was made in France, I believe," said Nancy. "If it's like the one I saw on the Internet."

"France sounds right. My family lived in Hampton, Virginia. Port town. Could have been traded there. Maybe one of my ancestors went to France and bought it. Wouldn't be surprised. I didn't see any date on it, did you?"

"But wasn't your family's jewelry store in Richmond?"

Grace shrugged. "Of course. We had relatives who worked at the port. Wasn't that far away." Grace sipped her tea. "I'm descended from travelers, you know. Could easily have brought that clock back after a visit to France."

Nancy nodded. "I'll go over it again, looking for a date." Grace seemed worried and tired, but perhaps the puzzle of the old clock would give her something else to think about. Nancy stood and Grace followed her to the door. "I'm not giving up yet," Nancy said, hugging Grace before she stepped out the door.

***

Nature Notes
by Anita Ferris

You are invited to a free lecture on "Protecting Our Birds," presented by Whisperwood's Audubon Circle. Pesticides, fewer habitats, feral cats, pollution—all are making life hard for our feathered friends. Find out how you can be part of the effort to keep birds singing in West Virginia. Wednesday, 7 p.m. Basement Classroom A. Refreshments will be served. Open to all.

- *The Whisperwood Breeze*

CHAPTER 11

That evening, Nancy met Fitz as he stepped out of his apartment, and they walked together down the hall to the dining room. Nancy had changed into gray slacks and pink sweater, and Fitz wore his customary jeans, white dress shirt, and tool belt. As they approached the dining room's reception desk, Nancy greeted her friends, Louise and George, holding hands which they occasionally did now. Louise's white slacks and white, long-sleeved turtleneck made her look like a house painter. She leaned on her cane.

George outshone them all in a fuchsia polo shirt and pink slacks. Fitz took one look at George and whistled. As usual, they were seated at table fifty-six, which was covered like all the other tables with a white linen tablecloth. Mauve napkins rolled around the silverware lay at each place.

Louise hung her cane on the chair back and groaned as she sat. "Been feeling pretty good until today, and just so you know, I'm wearing white 'cause I went out to check my hive before dinner. Bees like white—keeps 'em calm. My tip for the day."

George eyed her. "I have no intention of visiting your hives. Ever. No ma'am."

Fitz chuckled. "Mon, you've got to tell me how you choose your wardrobe. Who is your couturier?"

George sat up and preened himself like a cockatoo. "No one here dresses as well as I do."

"You're colorful," snickered Louise. "I'll say that for you."

George looked down at the sea of pinks he wore. "Yes," he said. "I am." He unrolled his mauve napkin and lined up the flatware beside his plate. "You may laugh, but I got sick of gray suits and conservative ties and swore that when I retired, I was going for color. I like color." He closed the subject by opening the menu.

The others took their cue, unwrapping the flatware and picking up the menus. After giving their orders to the server, Fitz spoke up in his Jamaican lilt. "I've been hearing stories, my friends, and I don't like what I'm hearing."

Louise again flicked her braid. "Me too, and I think we need to do something about it fast."

"I know," said Nancy, frowning. "We've all been hearing the stories. I got a phone call just a few minutes ago from Elizabeth Bowen, up on the fifth floor." Nancy shivered as she remembered the terror in Elizabeth's voice. "She said a bill collector called her and told her that her husband—he died three months ago—owed some company ten thousand dollars. If she didn't pay up by next Friday, he said the police would arrest her."

Louise leaned toward Nancy to peer around the pillar and survey the dining room. "Is she here anyplace? I don't see her."

"I thought I'd reassured her." Nancy also surveyed the dining room. "But I don't see her either."

Louise pursed her lips and frowned, folding her arms on the table. "She ought to know the police don't get involved in debt collection. Anyway, you don't go to jail for debt. Not since Charles Dickens' time." Louise turned to Nancy. "She's probably terrified to come out of her apartment. Go call her, Nancy. Tell her the caller was a crook. Tell her nobody is going to come after her, and she is not going to jail. Make sure she believes you this time."

Fitz looked up. "She can sit at our table if she wants. We'll protect her."

Nancy stood and scanned the dining room once more. "I'll do that right now. Of course you're right. I know that." She hurried out of the dining room to the house phone in the lobby, mentally kicking herself for not being on the ball. Poor Elizabeth.

Maria, Elvira, Vera, Elizabeth. Those were the victims Nancy had heard about. Louise knew others. Nancy tapped in Elizabeth's number. She heard it ring and ring. Was Elizabeth afraid to come to the phone? Nancy waited. Elizabeth finally answered with a trembling "Hello?"

She sounded like the perfect victim. Scared and vulnerable. With that response, she'd encourage any crook to go for the jugular. "Everything is all right," Nancy said in a firm voice. Someone had to have backbone. "You don't owe anyone anything."

"Nancy! I'm so glad it's you." Nancy heard a huge sigh of relief. "What did you say?"

"You were called by a thug trying to intimidate you." Nancy explained the law. "You're not the only one who's been threatened. Forget about it and come down to dinner." She added Fitz's suggestion. "You can join us. We'll protect you."

There was a long silence. Then Elizabeth quavered, "Are you sure? He said I owed money and had to pay. What about my credit rating?"

"He's a crook. You don't owe him anything. Come on down to dinner. Other people have gotten the same kind of call."

"They have?" Elizabeth still sounded hesitant. "You're sure?"

"Yes. I'm sure. Nobody will come after you." Elizabeth didn't say anything, so Nancy repeated her reassurance. "What they're saying is against the law. They've tried the same thing on others here." Why was Elizabeth so hard to convince even with all Nancy's reassurance? Most people were ready to accept her advice, especially if it got them off the hook.

"Thank you, Nancy. What a relief! I was sick with fear and afraid to leave my apartment." Elizabeth took a deep breath. "They knew his name. They knew he'd bought a new car just before he died. Said the debt was something to do with the car. I knew he'd paid up every cent owed on that car, but they knew about us, Nancy. This wasn't just some anonymous person calling a number out of a phone book. They picked me. Me!"

"You're not the only one who's been called," said Nancy. "But the scams are the same old scams crooks have been using for years. Don't worry. Come on down to dinner. We're working on this problem. If you get any more calls like that, just refer them to me. Tell them I'm your lawyer and need his name, address, and phone number." That should stop the calls, Nancy thought, and help Elizabeth gain the strength to stand up to the thug.

"I'll do it. And Nancy," she paused, "I'd sure like to see that guy in jail for scaring me. Let me know how I can help put them in prison." Nancy was about to hang up the phone when Elizabeth added, "for a long, long time."

As Nancy returned to her dinner companions, she again surveyed the dining room, this time looking for Alicia's tragic face. Nancy didn't see it and felt a slight misgiving, but Alicia could certainly have decided on a different time to eat or to go into town for dinner. Maybe she didn't feel like dinner at all. "What's going on, Nancy?" asked Fitz. "I saw Elizabeth just come in, and she's across the dining room talking and laughing. You must have told her the right thing."

Nancy glanced at him with a frown. "I did, but she said whoever it was brought up details about her life that only someone who knew her would know. Just one more bit of evidence that says whoever the crook is, he lives here."

Louise banged her fist on the table. "And we've got to find him fast. He terrifies people and might hit on someone vulnerable enough to try suicide."

Nancy brooded through the rest of the meal.

***

Keep Whisperwood Neat and Clean

> Complaints have been received about the clutter and messy appearance of some of the terrace apartments. Please remember your neighbors and help us maintain a clean and neat appearance. Whisperwood's regulations, drafted by your friends and neighbors on Whisperwood's Advisory Board, forbid the hanging of towels, bathing suits and other items on the balcony railings, any color other than white on the outside of window coverings such as draperies and shades, and the display of such items as flags and banners outside windows and balconies.
>
> *-Notice from the Residents' Advisory Board,*
> *The Whisperwood Breeze*

CHAPTER 12

The pedestal of the old clock, its porcelain case, and its inner workings lay scattered across Nancy's dining room table while she ate her morning breakfast cereal and stared at the pieces. Nancy could see nothing that would in any way be considered odd or different about the clock or its parts.

She replaced the inner workings, reset the clock onto its pedestal and returned it to the dressing table in her bedroom. She'd done her best. Time to bring in an expert.

She walked up the stairs to the library on the fifth floor and spent the morning poring over the three volumes of one-page autobiographies submitted by the residents. Really, she thought, I ought to have a set of these directories myself, considering how much use I make of them.

In the last volume, S-Z, she found a retired watchmaker. Stuart Zebrowski. Had she met him? Nancy studied his photo. She didn't think so. He lived on the opposite side of the building, near Betts' apartment, in fact.

Nancy reshelved the three volumes and returned to her apartment for lunch. Later that afternoon she set off to meet the watchmaker, hoping he'd be home and not away on some year-long jaunt.

As she approached his apartment, she heard the loud deep tones of a clock. She checked her watch at the second tone. Three o'clock. A third tone sounded. Nancy waited for more. None were forthcoming. The clock and her watch jibed. A good sign. Nancy knocked on the door.

She heard rattling within. Then a chair scraped and shuffling sounds grew louder as someone approached the door and opened it.

A bald man wearing a railroad cap, and the black-and-white striped jumpsuit of a railroad engineer stared out at her over glasses perched on his nose.

Nancy stepped back. "Mr. Zebrowski?"

"That's me. What can I do you for?"

"I need your help," Nancy said. "You've been a watchmaker, haven't you?"

Zebrowski stepped aside and waved her in. "Need a watch repair, do you?"

Nancy smiled, taking in the case clocks, mantel clocks, novelty clocks, and all the other clocks hanging on the walls and filling all the horizontal spaces. "This is fantastic," she said. "What a wonderful collection."

"Glad you like it. Take a seat." He gestured to a long wooden bench that doubled as a couch. Scratches and graffiti still showed through a coat of varnish "That's from the Baltimore station," he said and took a rocking chair for himself. "The wife didn't care for my collection, but she's gone now. Decided I might as well suit myself, you know."

"You have a clock museum here," said Nancy, smiling at him. "You could charge admission."

"You don't know the half of it." He grimaced. "More in storage." He pointed to several clocks in the form of cartoon figures. "Collectibles, those are. Disney characters and what not."

He nodded toward an austere clock in a plain oak case. "Seventeenth century, that one."

Nancy nodded in wonder. "You must know a lot about clocks. And watches, too."

"Yep. Started out on the railroad. Time's important to a railroad. When the railroads started crossing this country, that's when we began getting serious about time. Accurate time. Standardized time. Can't run a railroad without that. No sir." Zebrowski lazily rocked back and forth as he talked.

"Sounds like you know a lot about it," said Nancy. "When did you turn to watchmaking?"

"That's a whole 'nother story." Zebrowski was in no hurry, but Nancy was fascinated by the rhythmic ticking of such an assortment of clocks.

"Tell me about it," she said.

"My wife's daddy was a jeweler, and he needed someone he could count on to hang around, repair watches, and generally learn how to manage the business. I filled the bill and by that time was ready to quit the railroads. Tired of moving all the time, you know?"

Nancy nodded, thinking of Simon Smythe, another jeweler at Whisperwood who'd helped her solve her first case there. He was a totally different specimen from the rather benign appearance of Stuart Zebrowski.

Zebrowski stopped rocking and leaned forward. "So now what did you come to see me about?"

Nancy told him. "I thought if you would take a look at it, you might see something I've missed."

Zebrowski stood. "Well, then, young lady, let's go take a look."

***

Walking across the building to her apartment took every bit of patience Nancy possessed. On hind sight, she wished she'd taken the clock to him. Zebrowski limped along, one hand on the hall rail at every step. And then, of course, Zebrowski had to chat with acquaintances and friends he met along the way. Eventually, they arrived at Nancy's apartment. Nancy left him outside while she shooed Malone into the spare bedroom, then she ushered Zebrowski in.

"Coffee? Tea?" she asked as she gestured to the dining room table. He took one of the chairs, waving away the suggestion.

"Don't need nothing right now." He took out a pocket watch and glanced at it. "Getting close to dinner time. Can't afford any extra calories."

"Fine," said Nancy. She carried the clock out of the bedroom and set it in front of Stuart. "What do you think?"

He whistled. "Not to my taste, but it sure is fancy." He turned it around. "I've seen one of these before," he said. "Long time ago." He sat back and gazed off in the distance as he polished his glasses with a handkerchief dredged out of a pocket. "Auction. Brought in quite a pretty penny, it did. Imagine this would do the same."

He squinted up at Nancy. "Made just before the Civil War. France. Am I right?"

"I believe so." The old guy knew his stuff. "That's what I was told and what I found on the web. This particular clock is supposed to hold some kind of secret, though. Do you see anything odd about it?"

"Secret, huh?" Stuart chuckled. "You mean like a will? Money? Time is money, look in the clock. Something like that?" He snapped his fingers. "I got it. The secret leads to Confederate treasure." He chuckled again.

Nancy smiled. "I don't know. Take a good look at it. Tell me what you think."

Stuart nodded as he pulled a magnifying loupe out of his pocket and attached it to his glasses. "Let's see. . ." He took the clock off its pedestal. "Hmm. Made by Henri Marc, all right. About 1850, I reckon. Just before our Civil War." He looked up at Nancy. "Henri Marc was well-known back then. Parisian clockmaker. Nineteenth century. This here is what we call high-style rococo. Pretty, ain't it?" He took the working parts out of the clock case. "Silk thread suspension movement. Signed," he muttered to himself. He examined the case, probing the crevices and trying to move the flowers. He glanced up at Nancy. "Nothing secret there."

Then he examined the works through the loupe, removing a piece here, replacing it, removing another piece there and replacing it. He put the clock together again and stared at it.

Nancy stood next to him. "What about the clock face?" she asked. "Could there be something odd there?"

He glanced up at her. "You mean like a code? The dots marking the seconds spelling out Morse code? Something like that?"

Nancy nodded. That's exactly what she did mean.

"Nope. I don't see nothing odd or suggestive about this clock. It's a clock. A fancy one at that. Now, I'll tell you what I can do. I can make it keep time to the second if you let me take it for a week or so."

Nancy smiled. "Thank you. I appreciate that, but I don't think that's necessary. I'm just keeping it for a friend, trying to ferret out its secret."

"Too fancy for my taste." Stuart glanced at his watch. "Now I'm off to dinner. See you around."

He limped out the door. Nancy smiled, pleased to have met such a character who was such a resource—and pleased he didn't expect her to accompany him back down the hall.

***

A Gentle Request for Consideration

Whisperwood's Residents Committee has received a number of complaints about noise nuisances around the building that irritate, disturb or wake those in neighboring apartments. Barking dogs, over-loud televisions, clocks that tick loudly or chime at all hours, and the constant irritation of wind chimes are especially disruptive. We ask that all residents consider their neighbors and find ways to silence their dogs or chiming clocks and keep the volume down on their televisions. Wind chimes are not lovely to others. Please remove them from your balconies and terraces. Thank you.

Note From the Residents Committee,
The Whisperwood Breeze

CHAPTER 13

Tonight was filet mignon with onion rings night. When Nancy arrived at the dining room, it was more crowded than usual. One of the high school students serving there, Taneesha was beaming as she played host at the reception desk.

"Table fifty-six, as usual?" she asked. Her white blouse and black slacks shone crisp and clean under the black vest that indicated her three years in service.

Nancy smiled at her. "I'm a little early. Louise and George will be here in a few minutes. How are things, Taneesha?" Nancy asked. She liked Taneesha, who had proved an invaluable ally last year when they hunted a killer.

"I am so excited," Taneesha said, giggling as she picked up four menus. "I just got back from visiting West Virginia University. I think I'm going there next fall. I graduate in June, you know."

"That is wonderful," said Nancy. Taneesha was bright, curious, and industrious. She would go far, given a helping hand. Whisperwood's residents maintained a scholarship fund for the students who worked there. Nancy made a mental note to provide whatever additional help Taneesha would need. "What will you study?"

"After meeting you, what do you think?" Taneesha grinned.

Seeing Nancy's blank face, she added, "Criminal justice, of course."

Nancy laughed. "Of course. And you'll be excellent at it." Nancy followed her to table fifty-six, took the menu and watched Taneesha return to the reception desk. Criminal justice was a good field, but was it right for Taneesha? She was reliable, resourceful, and observant, all excellent qualities. Nancy hoped to be an inspiration, but not in that way. Still, four years of college allowed for a lot of experimentation and change. She decided not to worry about it. The great thing was that Taneesha was going to college.

Louise, George, and Fitz joined Nancy a few minutes later. Louise again wore white slacks and shirt. She slammed a thick manila envelope on the table as she sat. George jumped back, his blue polka-dotted bow tie wobbling against the top button of the bright red sports shirt he wore. Fitz stood behind him, dress shirt gleaming, jeans pressed. Nancy smiled at the three of them, amused at George's outfit and ever-thankful for Fitz's tool belt.

"We put out the request for people to submit instances of scams and scam attempts they've had while here at Whisperwood." Louise picked up the envelope and waved it. "These are the responses we've received so far."

George sat back and patted his stomach. "People been talking about it too." He dumped the silverware out of his napkin and laid the napkin across his lap. "A lot of people didn't even know they'd been scammed till they talked to other people here." He lifted up the fork and examined it.

Fitz watched him, shaking his head. "They do clean the silverware, George."

"He has to check everything," said Louise. She cast her eyes around the room, saw the dining room manager, signaled him, and then added, "I know there are a lot more victims we haven't heard from yet, though. Probably too embarrassed to come forward. If a bill collector was harassing you, you wouldn't talk about it, would you? Embarrassing, I would think."

Nancy saw the manager heading their way. Good. She'd like a glass of wine, too. Their server, like the other servers at Whisperwood, was a high school student and underage for serving alcohol. "After dinner, let's read through these. See what we've got." She perused the evening's menu. "We can do it in my apartment. It's closest."

Fitz opened his mouth. "Actually, my apartment is closer, don't you know? Just to set the record straight."

"You emptied those boxes yet?" asked Louise. "Last time we were there, I barely found a place to sit."

Fitz shook his head. "A lot to do here just keeping you and Nancy out of trouble."

Nancy laughed. "It's all right. My apartment is fine."

"Well, maybe," George grumbled. "If my dust allergies don't kick in."

Louise banged her spoon on the table. "Listen up, people. Harry told me the State Attorney's Office is lining up an expert on consumer fraud to come speak to us."

Nancy nodded. "Excellent, and going through the responses will help us steer the speaker to the scams that hit us seniors the most."

Nancy looked up to see the manager at her elbow. He asked his usual question. "How is everything?" After their reassurance, he smiled and bowed. "How may I help you?"

"Filet mignon tonight," George muttered before he looked up at the manager. "Merlot for me, please."

"Sure. Me too," said Louise. "I stay away from steak, though. And beef. Raising beef cattle is bad for the environment."

George sighed. "But it tastes so good."

"Wine for anyone else?" the manager asked, frowning at Louise.

Nancy and Fitz also agreed on the merlot, and the manager left, to be replaced by the server to take their menu selections.

"Heard from the tour organizers yet?" asked Louise.

Nancy shook her head. "Not yet."

"You going on a tour?" asked George with a glance at Louise. "Without me?"

Louise patted his arm. "Don't worry, George. It's a test Nancy roped me into, but of course you can come, too. Maine, New Brunswick, and Nova Scotia."

George and Fitz turned to Nancy. As she explained the tour's age discrimination policy, their salads arrived, and George picked up his fork. "Let's see what happens here first," he said, "before making any decisions."

After dinner, in Nancy's apartment, Louise opened the envelope and spilled the contents out on the dining room table. Malone wound himself around their feet, purring loudly. Nancy reached down to stroke his fur.

"Let's go through these and sort them," said Louise. "See what we have."

"There are so many." Nancy pulled a handful of responses out of the pile.

"Okay," said George, scanning through several sheets. "Here are some where they got calls supposedly from their grandson needing money to get out of a Mexican jail." He read through the responses. "Most of them were smart enough to check first, but here's one who did send money and only found out later that her grandson was actually in Florida with his other grandparents."

"Put all those in this pile." Louise pointed to a fledgling pile. "I'm starting a pile for people who got e-mails supposedly from friends who'd been robbed and needed money to get back home."

"And I have a pile here from people who got calls or e-mails from a bill collector or the IRS. Quite a crock, actually." Fitz's bifocals slid down his nose as he read, shaking his head. "Why would they fall for this stuff?"

"Anybody get millions from a Nigerian prince?" asked George.

Louise laughed. "That one has been around too long. I've been looking for victims of a pigeon drop scam, but I don't think Whisperwood lends itself to that one."

"What's that?" asked Fitz.

"Somebody comes up to you and says they've found a package full of money and will split it with you, but first. . ."

"Oh yeah." Fitz nodded. "I remember that one."

"Most of the Whisperwood residents would remember faces they see in the halls even if they don't know the name or anything else about the person," said Nancy. "Hard to disappear with ill-gotten loot if you tried that kind of scam here."

"Those scams can originate anywhere in the world. Nigeria seems to be a popular place for them."

"Yeah," said George. "Usually the scammers don't speak or write English well and make enough grammatical and spelling errors to turn most of us off. But the scam pitches aimed at the residents here seem to be more literate. No one mentions a phone caller having a foreign accent."

Louise nodded. "We're just a small town," She waved a hand to indicate the entire building. "And someone here knows enough about us to make these scamming pitches believable."

"The question is, who?" muttered George.

Nancy had trouble concentrating on the task at hand when every time she looked up she saw the desk and remembered the letter. George, Louise, and Fitz were her closest friends. Could she ask them? She cleared her throat. "I'd like your advice," she began hesitatingly. Under the table, Malone growled. Even he had a problem with that letter, Nancy thought.

Louise looked up from the forms on the table. "Sure, Nancy, what's the problem?"

Fitz sat back in his chair. "Anything, my darlin'."

Nancy frowned at him. "I received a letter a week ago. . ."

"Uh oh," said George. "Blackmail. I can smell it." He narrowed his eyes. "What have you done, Nancy?"

Louise slapped his hand. "Nobody would have anything to blackmail Nancy about."

Nancy could have contradicted Louise but chose not to. *Let the past stay buried. Hard enough just to talk about the letter.* She shook her head. "Not blackmail. Just some disturbing news. I'm puzzled and upset and don't know what to do about it." She glanced at her hands, folded on the table. "And I don't know how I feel about it."

"So tell us," said Louise, "and we'll tell you how to feel about it. No problem."

Nancy smiled. "You see, Bill and I, we met twenty years ago. I'd been single for many years after my first husband died, and Bill swept me off my feet."

"I knew Bill," put in Fitz. "He and Malone had a great act. He was a good man. Good magician too. "

Nancy nodded and said softly, "Yes, he was." Her voice quavered, and she swallowed as she pushed back the tears. She refused to cry. "I thought I knew everything about him, you see, but now I don't know. . ."

"So what does the letter say?" demanded Louise. "Was he a wife beater? Ex-Offender? Murderer? Spy? What did he do?"

Nancy stared down at the table and spoke in a low voice. "I knew he'd been married before, and from everything he said, he and his first wife had a loving and close relationship. However," Nancy took a deep breath, "according to the letter, he must have had an affair." She stopped and took a sip of wine.

There was a stunned silence.

"The letter wasn't anonymous, was it?" asked Louise, frowning with narrowed eyes.

Nancy shook her head. She felt her eyes again tearing up. She steeled herself against her emotions. "Bill and his wife did not have children, but . . ." Nancy took a deep breath. "That letter is from someone who claims to be his daughter, born to another woman while Bill was still married to his first wife. The daughter wants to meet me." There. Now that she'd said it, the letter seemed less threatening. She still felt betrayed. Why hadn't Bill told her? She had checked his background when they were dating. She was a detective, for goodness sake. That's what she did. She had found no red flags. Of course, nothing like an affair and an illegitimate daughter would show up in her sources. All hushed up, of course.

"But why does she want to meet you now?" asked Louise. "Maybe she got it all wrong. Maybe her mother made up that story. You don't know."

"If you ask me," put in George, "and you did, this could just be another scam. In fact, it probably is. All you have is a letter. She probably wants money."

George was right. Nancy took a deep breath. It could just be a scam. If she hadn't been so upset at reading the letter, she would have done some checking on the writer. And that's what she should do now.

Memories of Bill dashed through her mind. She had met him at a friend's home and he changed her life. She would never forget her first husband, a loving, kind man. They'd known each other since school days. Living with him had been placid and comfortable. He had supported her in her career as she had supported him in his.

After he died, she had lived a full and exciting life as a single woman, then Bill exploded into her life and it became a whirlwind that only calmed down when they retreated to their West Virginia cabin. Even there, though, they were often surrounded by friends and the whirlwind continued. *Hard to catch your breath with Bill.* She could imagine how that expressive personality, that consummate entertainer, would attract women, but how would he respond? Until the letter, she would have felt confident that he would not respond, that he would be faithful to her.

She clung to her memories. Theirs had been a happy marriage. She had not known it rested on sand.

"Okay," said Louise, "the first thing you do is check her out. Does she have a criminal record? History of mental illness. Who is she and who, exactly, are her parents?"

"Then," added Fitz, "if she checks out all right, you invite her here for lunch. You can either talk with her alone or you can have one of us along. Whatever you need."

"And after that," said Louise, "you come to my apartment and tell me all about it. That's the way to put this problem to rest."

She laid her hand on Nancy's arm and looked her in the eye. "You hear me?"

Nancy nodded. "Yes, I hear you." They were right. She should check her out and then ask her to lunch. Nancy dabbed a tissue on her eyes and smiled at her friends. If all this ended badly, she had backup.

***

Let Us Learn Who You Are

Many fascinating people live at Whisperwood, and some of you have led adventurous lives. Please tell us about yourself. We've noticed that the residents' directories are missing the biographies of some of our residents. Please check the directory to make sure your page is present and up to date, including your photo. We'd like to know who you are. Bio sheets make it easy. Just fill in the blanks and return the sheet to the receptionist in the lobby. She will take your photo and add it to your bio and then put it in the appropriate directory. The directories are available to all in the fifth floor library.

- *The Whisperwood Breeze, Newsletter for Whisperwood Retirement Village*

CHAPTER 14

No one could say living at Whisperwood was boring, Nancy thought as she walked to the opposite wing of the Whisperwood main building. Con artists were targeting the residents, one resident had been murdered, and she had been attacked three times. Three times. She paused and looked behind her, feeling relieved to find the hall empty. She must pose a threat to whoever it was, but why? What were they afraid she'd do? What would they try next?

Louise was right. She better keep her wits about her, stay around other people, and not drive to town until they found out what this was all about.

Other than hearing that the sheriff had interviewed a few residents, Nancy knew of no action from the sheriff toward solving Betts' murder. She hadn't even seen him around the building. What was he doing? Should she take the shuttle into town and talk with him? Would he tell her anything if she did?

Nancy climbed the stairs to the sixth floor and sought out Betts' apartment. She stopped at each landing to catch her breath, but she liked the exercise. Then she opened the stairwell door and stepped out into a mirror image of her own hallway, with cheerful, personal displays on the hall shelves by each door. Nancy stopped at each display, reading and admiring the awards, certificates, family photos, medals, or bowls of candy and tried to imagine the person it represented. She pulled out a pad and pen and noted the names on the doors as she passed them. She'd read their biographies in the resident directories later, then maybe she'd try to find out what they might know about Betts.

Ruth Smith lived in an apartment next to Betts'. Nancy searched her memory. Had she met Ruth Smith? Surely she would remember such an unmemorable name and thought that perhaps they had played bridge together occasionally. Ruth had set out photos of grandchildren and a wedding portrait for her display. On the other side of Betts' apartment, a Reverend Charles Hilliard lived. A half-empty bowl of jelly beans sat on his shelf. Nancy smiled and took a couple of jelly beans as she knocked on his door.

She heard movement inside and the shuffling of papers, then the door opened. A tall, bald, lantern-jawed gentleman in blue polo shirt and black slacks peered at her. "Am I late?" he asked.

Nancy glanced behind her. "I don't know," she said. "For what?"

"You're not here to pick me up?" He seemed flustered. "I'm sorry. Come in, come in."

He stepped aside and took her by the arm, maneuvering her around a bag of golf clubs and steering her into the living room.

"What do you need?" he asked. "I don't do pastoral counseling anymore."

Nancy stepped away from his arm. "I'm not here for counseling." She looked around the austere room. An overlarge brown armchair dominated the living room. It stood on the white wall-to-wall carpet next to a lamp and a table covered with stacks of papers and books. Two plain kitchen chairs faced the armchair.

"Have a seat," said Hilliard as he took the armchair. "Now

what's troubling you?" He glanced at his watch. "We have a few minutes."

He reminded Nancy of the white rabbit in *Alice in Wonderland.* "I was hoping to talk with Betts Horner's roommate," she said, sitting in one of the kitchen chairs. Hard and uncomfortable. Was this how he shortened his counseling sessions? She smiled at the thought.

Hilliard steepled his hands and stared up at the ceiling as if he were reminiscing. "So sad. Such a nice lady." He waved toward the door. "She lived next door, not here."

"She was a nice person. I wish I'd known her better." Nancy took a deep breath. "I'm helping the police with their investigation into her death." Ambrose would flip if he heard that, but chances were, he'd never find out. "Can you tell me anything about her?"

Hilliard sat back and studied Nancy through half-closed eyes. "I remember now. You're that private eye person who moved in here awhile back. I've heard about you."

Nancy nodded. Hilliard didn't sound impressed. Had Ambrose talked with him or did he have outmoded ideas of what women should do? She'd met those kind before, and she could pull out her sweet little old lady act if she needed to.

"So you're not here for counseling," he said, adjusting his position in the chair as if it adjusted his ideas, too.

"I don't know what I can tell you," he went on. "She tried to be helpful and a good neighbor. She liked the idea of being next to a minister, even if I was Lutheran and she'd been raised Methodist."

He retreated into himself for a moment. "Not practicing though," he muttered, then looked back at Nancy. "Still, she was a nice lady. Even brought over cookies once." A faint smile crossed his face and his eyes gazed off at something distant. "Can't imagine why anyone would want to kill her." He shook his head. "And here of all places. Terrible world."

Nancy probed. "What was she like?"

Hilliard shook his head. "Spoke her mind but smart. Shrewd. I could see that in her. I don't think much got past her."

Nancy compared his assessment with her own. She had only met Betts once. Grace had dominated the conversation, but Betts' comments were shrewd bordering on sarcastic. "No enemies? Anyone have a grudge against her? Did she carry large amounts of cash with her? Wear expensive jewelry?"

Hilliard waved a hand. "Why would she carry cash around with her in this place? No reason. Wouldn't recognize expensive jewelry if I saw it."

Nancy nodded. The man didn't have the faintest idea what Betts would or would not do. "What about her roommate?" she asked. "Did they get along? What is she like?"

"Her roommate." He paused, pushing his lips in and out. Finally, he looked at Nancy and shook his head. "They certainly did not get along. Different kettle of fish and that's all. Had her own personality as we all do." He paused and contemplated the door. "Don't get me wrong. Both were nice people, good neighbors."

Interesting. Nancy looked forward to meeting the roommate. "Do you have any thoughts or suggestions about what happened to Betts?"

"Can't imagine. Might as well kill me as her. No reason. No reason at all, but then," he leaned forward, his fingers stabbing at Nancy, "there's never a good reason for murder."

Nancy rose, thanked him for his help, and left. She strode past Betts' apartment to Ruth Smith's place on the other side. She knocked on the door as she gazed at the family photos on the hall shelf.

The door opened, and a tall, thin woman in purple suit-dress with shoulder-length straight gray hair stared out at Nancy. "Yes?"

Nancy introduced herself, looking up into Ruth's face. "I'm helping Sheriff Ambrose with his investigation," she added. In with a penny, in with a pound. Ambrose would never know. "I'd like to ask you a few questions about Betts Horner, your neighbor."

The woman opened the door wider and stepped aside. "Come in. I'm Ruth Smith," she said in a soft, southern drawl. "I was the first person she met here. She was a nice person. Her roommate too. Both nice people."

Nancy walked into another white carpeted living room. How prevalent white carpeting was at Whisperwood, Nancy thought, a luxury made possible because the mud and dirt were scraped off at the lobby doors and the residual rubbed off just walking in the halls. The couch and armchairs were upholstered in white with a pastel flower design. An exuberant philodendron stretched along a set of low shelves to frame the large window at the end of the living room.

Ruth still stood at the door, arms folded, watching her. "Now you know," she said, "I don't believe you're helping Sheriff Ambrose. I think you're here on your own."

Nancy froze and then turned to look at her. Before she could think of a response, Ruth added, "But that's quite all right. I don't trust him to do a good job either. Please, take a seat." Ruth stood aside and waved at a chair. "Elected without any law enforcement credentials at all. Would you like some tea?"

Tea. She could dawdle, but Ruth was no dummy. She seemed cooperative, though. "I would love some, thank you."

Ruth stepped into the kitchen while Nancy sank into an armchair. Quite comfortable, especially when compared with the reverend's hard wooden kitchen chairs. Nancy noted the paintings on the wall. They were well-done portraits, probably family. Had Ruth painted them? She could see into the den, each wall covered with floor to ceiling bookcases, each shelf filled with books.

Ruth brought out a tray with two cups and a teapot covered by a woolen cozy. As Ruth set the tray down on the coffee table, Nancy could see sugar cubes in a silver bowl. She hadn't seen sugar cubes since she was a child.

Ruth poured and handed Nancy the cup. Both of them added several sugar cubes to the cups. Ruth smiled. "I see you like sugar as much as I do."

Nancy laughed. "Long-time habit." She sat back and took a sip. "Have you lived here long?" asked Nancy. She couldn't remember meeting Ruth anywhere.

"About six years." Ruth sipped her tea. "How about you?"

"Almost a year. Moved here from Morgantown."

Ruth slapped a hand against her forehead. "Oh my yes. You're that private investigator, aren't you?"

Nancy grimaced. "Long time ago. Retired."

Ruth peered at Nancy over the tea cup. "No wonder you're interested in what happened to Betts. We're all worried about a murderer on the loose here."

"I thought my skills would come in handy." Nancy paused, wanting to reel this fish in slowly. "I only met Betts once, but I liked her. She was an intelligent and interesting person."

"She was. I can't imagine why anyone would kill her." Ruth shook her head. She reached for a tissue and blew her nose.

"Did she have any enemies? Anyone hold a grudge against her?"

Ruth hesitated, her cup inches from her lips. A flash of anger crossed her face. She looked at Nancy. "I'm from Oxford, Mississippi. Now I know what people say about Mississippi, but my daddy taught us to respect everyone no matter what their color or occupation. I liked Betts. She was good people, quality people. She didn't deserve what happened to her. She did not.'

Nancy nodded. "I agree. Do you think she might have been

killed because she was African-American?"

"A lot of good ol' boys live around here." Ruth frowned. "Them and their pick-up trucks and Confederate flags. I do not respect ignorant louts. West Virginia was a Union state, I guess you know. The people in this state with their small farms and corn liquor were ripped off by the owners of those big slave-driven plantations who made the laws to suit themselves. West Virginians cut their own throats if they supported the Confederacy."

Having met pick-up trucks sporting Confederate flags driven recklessly and at high speeds on the county roads, Nancy had her own opinion about ignorant louts. "But Betts was murdered at Whisperwood. I haven't seen much of that kind of prejudice here." Except from Jefferson, but he was an odd fish, and he had an agenda.

Ruth took another sip of tea. "You wouldn't," she said slowly. "Prejudice is subtle here and coated with patronizing and fawning. Easy to miss and easy to mistake."

Nancy knew prejudice existed at Whisperwood. She'd met people who in a fit of pique would use the horrible "N" word with their friends and then fawn over the African-American staff in the dining room. She had considered racism to be reprehensible and ugly but impotent at Whisperwood. "I haven't met her roommate," Nancy said to move beyond the swamp of prejudice. "What is she like?"

"She's just delightful," said Ruth. "I enjoy talking with her. She paints too." Ruth waved at the paintings on the wall.

"You painted those?" said Nancy, although she'd already guessed that. "They're lovely."

"Thank you." Ruth smiled with pride shining in her eyes. "Now that it's spring, Samira and I are taking our art projects outdoors and painting landscapes."

"I've heard that Samira and Betts didn't get along," Nancy said.

"Of course they had squabbles." Ruth frowned as she sipped her tea. "You live together, you're not going to agree on everything. Fact of life."

Mere squabbles was not what Nancy had heard.

"Betts didn't like the smell of the paints, but I showed Samira where to stow her painting supplies and unfinished work in the arts and crafts room in the basement." Ruth beamed at Nancy. "Then it became no problem."

A wave of bad memories swept through Nancy's mind at the mention of the basement. Tied up with her friends, afraid for her life. She rarely went down there any more. She set her teacup on the tray and rose.

"I'm glad I met you," said Nancy. "Thank you for talking with me and thank you for the tea."

"Surely no one here killed Betts," Ruth said as she walked Nancy to the door. "It must have been an accident—some hunter in the woods, maybe, getting off a sound shot."

"Sound shot?"

"You know. Hearing a sound and shooting at it? Some of those hunters are irresponsible with no imagination. A sound shot. That's what it must have been. I can't believe there's a murderer here."

Nancy walked back to her own apartment, mulling over Ruth's comments. They had been subtly conflicting, as if to test Nancy, gently pushing her one way, then another. Was that simply her manner or did she have some other agenda? Ruth was deeper than she appeared.

As Nancy approached her apartment, she heard Malone scampering across the floor. She walked in and saw the cat batting at a letter someone had pushed under the door. Nancy chased Malone and grabbed it out of his grasp. It was addressed to her but had no stamp. Expecting an invitation or announcement, Nancy slid the letter out of the envelope and scanned it. Then she read it more carefully.

It was a well-written request to stop all inquiries into the "so-called scams, which are actually nothing more than a legitimate way to conduct business." Nancy almost laughed. The letter was signed "A resident." She looked over the envelope. No clues to who had sent the letter. Would there be fingerprints?

She set the letter down, went to a drawer and returned with a small jar. She sprinkled powder from the jar onto the letter and gently blew the powder across the paper. She brought the lamp closer and angled it. There were several prints on the edges where Nancy had held the letter, but no other prints appeared. Just to be sure the prints were her own, Nancy brought out a magnifying glass and studied them. She knew her own prints and the ones on the letter were definitely hers, tiny scars and all. Whoever wrote the letter had worn gloves.

A veiled threat concluded the letter. "We honest citizens at Whisperwood will have to take further action if your unwanted intrusion into our private affairs continues."

Nancy called Louise.

"An anonymous letter?" Louise said. "And a preposterous premise. Ridiculous. Pay no attention, Nancy." She paused, then in a more querulous voice added, "You don't suppose it carries some kind of poison or germ, do you? Like anthrax?"

"I certainly hope not, since both Malone and I have touched it. So far, the culprit's attempts to silence me could have been considered accidents."

"I don't think so. That cut brake line wasn't subtle."

"Maybe not, but it probably wouldn't have been discovered unless someone examined my car after we ran off the road," said Nancy, glancing again through the letter. "Is the local sheriff up to that? Anyway, anthrax just seems a bit too sophisticated for whoever is attacking me, but who could that be?"

"Someone who doesn't have all his marbles," Louise said. "I don't think they have a leg to stand on. Everyone I've talked to about the upcoming talk has been eager and excited to hear it. If the letter writer does think he has a case and support, let him send the board a petition. At least he sent a letter and not a box of poisoned chocolates. We'd all better start watching out for that now."

***

Acrylic Painting Class
Begins Next Tuesday

Whisperwood's award-winning artist, Ruth Smith, will teach a beginning class in acrylic panting beginning next Tuesday at 10 a.m. in the Arts & Crafts classroom in the basement. Unlike oil paints, acrylic paints have little smell and dry fast. They are ideal for apartment living. Cost is $10 plus a $25 materials fee. You must register by Friday at the front desk so Ruth can acquire enough painting materials for everyone.

- *The Whisperwood Breeze, Newsletter for Whisperwood Retirement Village*

CHAPTER 15

Nancy visited Samira the next morning, introducing herself as Grace's concerned neighbor.

Samira waved aside Nancy's explanation as she invited Nancy into the apartment. Betts' roommate looked haggard as if she hadn't slept in days and her eyes were red. From weeping? She carried a tissue in her hand and a box of tissues lay on the coffee table.

She, too, was African-American, light-skinned with hair shaven close to her head, a risky style but her ears were small and dainty with a pearl in each lobe. She wore a tailored sea-blue caftan that showed off her figure. The woman was stunning. She could have been a model in her younger years.

Nancy realized she was staring open-mouthed. She stammered a greeting.

Samira nodded, amused. "I've heard of you. Welcome." She gestured for Nancy to follow her into the apartment. "Have a seat. Coffee? It's Ethiopian, where coffee was first discovered. Brought back from my last trip."

"Really? Ethiopian? I'd love some." It was Nancy's policy to accept what was offered, but she preferred tea. Still, coffee from Ethiopia was worth a try.

"Are you from Ethiopia?" she asked.

"I'm from southern Virginia," Samira said. "Where my ancestors came from is, I'm afraid, lost in history." She said it without rancor. "But I've traveled in Ethiopia. When they serve coffee, it's quite a ceremony."

Nancy glanced around the room. An African theme dominated. The mahogany chairs and couch were covered with cushions depicting giraffes, hippos, and rhinos in patterns of black, yellow, and green. The crowded bookshelves displayed wooden sculptures from Africa as well. Nancy sat on the couch under a large painting of circles repeating the African colors that hung on the wall.

Samira came out with two cups on a tray with cream and sugar. "Now. What can I do to help you?"

"I am so sorry for your loss," Nancy began as she pushed aside several glass animal figures on the coffee table so Samira could set the tray down.

Samira added cream and sugar to a cup. "Thank you." She handed the cup to Nancy.

"Do you have any idea who would have done such a thing?" Nancy asked. "I'm helping Sheriff Ambrose with his investigation."

Samira glanced at Nancy and smiled. "I doubt that," she said, then seeing Nancy's expression, she flicked her hand. "Don't worry. I won't blow your cover." She sipped her coffee. "As it happens, I have no faith in Sheriff Ambrose. He is lost here, but he's going through the motions." She lifted an eyebrow. "As best he can."

Nancy nodded. "Yes, he is. I'm afraid he'll bumble along until he can pin it on someone, anyone."

Samira smiled. "I see we are of one mind."

"Who do you think might have done it?" asked Nancy.

"I don't know. Jefferson sounds like the most likely suspect." Samira took another sip of coffee. "Or maybe his wife."

"Did anyone have a grudge against Betts?"

Samira cast an amused glance at Nancy. "She was black, you know. That's all some people need." She leaned back in her chair. "Putting obvious racism aside, Betts wasn't everyone's cup of tea. She was outspoken and shrewd and . . . tough. She'd been a cop, you know, years ago. Then she went into computer security. She knew something was going on around here, and she was trying to find out who was behind it."

Nancy struggled to keep her face blank. Here was a real clue. A concrete reason someone might want to kill Betts. "What did she think was going on?"

Samira stared into her cup. "I'm not sure," she said at last. "Things had become so tense between us that we were barely speaking." She looked directly at Nancy. "I'll tell you this. Betts came in one afternoon, laughing so hard she could barely get the words out. Something about an old clock and how some bastard—that's the word she used—thought it held a secret to Confederate treasure." Samira lifted an eyebrow and shrugged. "Can you imagine it? Confederate treasure in a clock? Guess I'd laugh too."

"What could be so funny about a clock, even if it did hold the secret to Confederate treasure? Did she explain that at all?" Nancy took another sip of the strong dark brew. "Why was she laughing?"

Samira shook her head. "I have no idea. She refused to talk about it or explain anything, and I don't know what clock she was talking about."

"How odd." Nancy's mind buzzed with possibilities but nothing made any sense. How would Betts know anything about Grace's clock? Betts and Grace hadn't even met before they both moved to Whisperwood. "Do you think the clock had anything to do with what Betts was investigating?"

Samira shook her head. "Betts was looking into something criminal going on here and happened on the clock by accident. Anyway, what would be funny about that?"

Nancy agreed. Nothing was funny about cheating elderly people out of their savings. What if Betts had found out who was behind the scam operation? Would she have confronted them and then they killed her?

"Do you know what she'd found out so far?"

Samira shook her head. "Afraid not. She didn't confide in me."

"She might have notes on her computer." Nancy glanced around the room. She didn't see any electronics except the large, flat-screen television.

"Sheriff went over her computer—I knew her password and could get him in, but I don't think he knew what he was doing."

That fit with what Nancy knew about Ambrose. He wouldn't call in a state expert either, preferring to act like an expert when he clearly was not.

Samira sipped her coffee, then went on. "The sheriff didn't find anything, so after he left, I also went through her files and her history cache. Nothing there that looked at all suspicious, incriminating, or relevant to what's been happening here."

Samira shrugged. "So Betts' sister took the computer for one of the kids. I think she deleted all the files—didn't want the kids to see anything they shouldn't." Samira poured more coffee into her cup. "She apologized for taking it, as if I'd object. Hell, I've got my own computer, didn't need Betts." She nodded at a laptop on the dining room table.

"They knew we didn't get along." Samira hesitated. "Actually, I was planning to move out. We'd been good friends before we moved here, worked together, you know, in cyber security. Pals on and off the job, but we didn't do well living in the same apartment."

"That's all changed," Nancy said. "Are you going to stay here?"

Samira frowned. "Still thinking about it."

Nancy didn't mind being nosy. "So will you pay whoever inherits her property for her half of the apartment?"

Samira gazed down into her cup a moment before replying. "We made wills when we bought into Whisperwood. Just in case, you know."

Nancy nodded.

"So we each included a codicil that in the event of the demise of one of us, the other one would inherit the other half of the apartment. Made it easier—neither one of us had kids or husbands." Samira sat back, stretched an arm out across the back of the couch, and crossed her legs. She looked at Nancy with a half smile. "So I guess that makes me a prime murder suspect."

***

Nancy left Samira's apartment and walked down the six flights of stairs to the first floor. She couldn't see Samira as the killer. Samira and Betts had worked together in security and must have had similar ethical and moral values. At least, that ought to be the case. Probably went through security checks themselves.

Were they involved in the fight against drug trafficking? She supposed there might be Whisperwood residents involved in illegal drugs. She knew of several alcoholics. A possibility.

Slave trafficking? No one here had servants who might be working against their will, and Harry Doyle and the Whisperwood Board would not engage in anything illegal. Smuggling? Whisperwood was a few miles off the Interstate, but smuggling would still be difficult at Whisperwood with its battalion of security guards and nosy residents. Theft? The stories and rumors of lost valuables had stopped with the capture of the culprits last year.

The criminal activity now taking place at Whisperwood was the proliferation of scamming attacks on the residents. Had Betts discovered the culprits? Is that why she was murdered? Was Samira in danger? Everyone knew Nancy had been a private detective. Were the scammers behind the attempted rundown of Nancy in the parking lot? The black widow spider incident or the cut brake line ? What would they try next?

***

Whisperwood Federal Credit Union
Offers all financial services
Loans
Investments
Checking and savings accounts
Safety deposit boxes
Come talk to one of our
friendly representatives today!
Located next to the main lobby
reception desk.

Ad in The Whisperwood Breeze

Chapter 16

On the first floor, Nancy took the side exit and walked out into a day brilliant in sunshine. And warm. Samira's apartment, as beautifully decorated as it was, had felt claustrophobic as more details about Betts surfaced. Nancy needed fresh air..

She walked down the path that circled the main building, calling to Whisperwood's two Rottweilers, Ham and Eggs, lolling about in the grass. They came running to her, and she knelt down to pet them. After the terrible situation at Whisperwood the summer before, they had been allowed to wander freely on the property during the day and confined at dusk to their pen at the gate. The residents paid them so much attention and gave them so many treats, the dogs remained close to home most of the time. Nancy liked dogs and might have adopted one if Malone hadn't adopted her and Bill first, and he had seen the potential for Malone in his magic act.

Memories of Bill and their cabin in the West Virginia woods threatened to overwhelm Nancy, and she hugged Ham as Eggs nuzzled in for attention.

"Mighty fine dogs."

Nancy's eyes followed the mahogany cane up to its owner, Jefferson, who stood there in white slacks and pale blue guayabera. No string tie today. She gave Ham and Eggs each a pet as she rose stiffly from her kneeling position. "How are you, Jefferson."

"Just fine, this splendid day, thank you." Jefferson leaned on his cane with both hands. "Where are you off to?"

"I'm going over to see what's happening at the garden. Have you been there yet?" Nancy didn't trust Jefferson but wanted to be friendly. She smiled at him and brushed off her hands.

"I'll join you, if I may," said Jefferson, turning in the direction of the path. "Where is it?"

"Come along. It's for the residents, and they often furnish the kitchen here with fresh produce and herbs." Nancy walked alongside Jefferson, slowing her pace to match his. What if he were the murderer? Or the scammer? Was she in danger here? She looked down at the two dogs trotting alongside, tongues hanging out.

Jefferson stopped and bent over several times to pet the dogs, murmuring, "Wish I had some treats for you two, good boys, good boys." He looked up at Nancy and smiled. "Love dogs. Always have. Always will."

The dogs lapped up the attention. Maybe the dogs were some protection, but she could stay on the path. A lot of people walked the path, especially on a beautiful morning like this.

Jefferson groaned as he straightened his back. "Had my knee replaced six months ago—before I came here." He brandished his cane. "Hoped I'd be through with this nuisance by now."

"You're doing quite well," said Nancy. "How's Helen?"

He snorted. "She's still in bed. Refused to get up this morning, but I opened our window and looked out at this fine meadow, sparkly with dew, warm breezes wafting in over my body, and I said to myself, I've got to get out in that. It's just like a spring day in Richmond." He sighed.

Nancy hadn't expected such a poetic sentiment from a man she'd come to regard as a bigot and a racist. Live and learn. "It does feel lovely. I'd hate to miss this, too."

"Makes me want to recite poetry," said Jefferson.

Really, the man could be disarming. Nancy continued leading Jefferson down the path, turning off onto a trail that disappeared behind the building. "The garden's this way."

Up ahead she could see the high chain-link fence that surrounded the residents' community garden. A shed stood at one corner. Nancy looked beyond the fence area to see the single bee hive, a square white column almost as tall as Louise, who stood next to it, covered by the white bee suit and helmet with netting coming down over her shoulders. She held the hive cover in hands covered by tough yellow rubberized gloves. A few bees buzzed around her as she laid aside the cover and looked into the hive. It was constructed of four layers resting on a platform. Each layer was a square wooden box with the bottom box about twelve inches high and the others about six inches high.

"Whoa," said Jefferson, shuddering. "I don't want to get involved in that."

"Don't worry." Nancy waved at Louise, who had just looked up. She waved back. "Louise says they're gentle bees and won't attack unless you mess with them. They're not even attacking her."

"I certainly am not going to mess with them. No sir." Jefferson backed away.

"Let's go see what's growing in the garden," said Nancy, opening the gate into the garden plots while pushing the dogs aside to keep them out. Inside the fence, garden plots were marked off in ten-foot squares, bounded by a narrow path. Each plot had its own individual character devised by its owner. In some, welcoming signs and bird feeders hung from trellises.

"Tomatoes are popular. Peas and beans, too," Nancy said. "People are just setting them out." She smiled at a woman in a straw hat, long-sleeved shirt, and corduroy pants carrying a flat of seedlings down the garden path. "Not quite past the frost date yet," the woman said with a grin, "but I'm a risk-taker."

"My folks had a farm once," said Jefferson as he surveyed the plots. "Grew tobacco and corn, usual stuff. Hard work." He pushed his lips in and out as he gazed across the garden. "Brings back memories, this does."

Nancy stopped at a plot that seemed devoted to herbs. She identified young seedlings of rosemary, thyme, oregano, basil and parsley. She didn't recognize another grouping of plants, although there was one resembling a plant she knew to cause severe gastric upsets. Why would anyone grow such a thing here? Maybe it had other uses as well. She studied the other unknown plants to look up later. Whose plot was this? The plot owner wasn't identified.

Jefferson hobbled on around the plots. Nancy watched him admire a bird house here and a garden troll there. Finally, he turned, spied Nancy, and walked toward her. "Takes me back, it does," he said. "Takes me back."

Nancy glanced at him with softer eyes. The man had some kind of soul. "Did you and Grace grow up together?" she asked.

"We're related, but don't put us in the same envelope," Jefferson said, "so to speak. We didn't see each other much till we moved here. She was the daughter of my father's younger sister. His sister, my aunt, of course, married a bad 'un, and so our folks didn't have much to do with each other after that."

"What do you mean, 'bad 'un'?" Nancy glanced at Jefferson. What was behind those words? Jealousy? Spite? Rivalry? Just plain nastiness? Whatever her parents were like, Grace seemed like a pleasant person to Nancy.

"Now, I'm not the one to go 'round telling tales." He shook his head and squinted at Nancy in the bright sunlight. "Besides, it's all old family history, but my folks always said her folks stole the family heirlooms from them, so that means they rightly belong to me, but now Grace has them, that I do know, however she got them. If she were a true Southern woman who respected the South and its traditions, she'd return them to me." He pursed his lips. "Yes sir. That's what she'd do."

"I see," said Nancy. Not much substantial there at all and certainly not Grace's fault. Any of it.

"The problem is, you see," Jefferson stopped to look at Nancy. "Grace doesn't have any children, so who's she going to leave that stuff to? A neighbor? Or the state? It should stay in the family. My wife and I have two children to carry on our name. That's who should get the family heirlooms. It's not fair that she has them and it's not fair how she got them. That's how it is, Nancy." He pounded his cane on the path. "Grace refuses to listen to reason, so we don't know what's going to happen. She may even sell them."

"I only met Grace's husband Richard once," said Nancy to change the subject. "He is always out somewhere. He must be quite a golfer."

"She doesn't seem to have much luck with marriage." Jefferson walked along, poking his cane at flowers that caught his interest. "This one's the third. One died on her and the other ran off with her car and her best friend. Didn't make it though." Jefferson paused and stared out at the woods.

"What happened to him?" Nancy asked.

"You could say his just desserts." Jefferson grinned at Nancy. "He ran the car off the road and killed both him and his girlfriend on their way out of town."

They walked along silently for a few minutes. Nancy processed this last bit of information. No wonder Grace was so obstinate about her possessions. She had lost so much in her life. "Richard seems to be attentive to her." Nancy didn't know that but hoped it was a reasonable assumption.

"I suppose so." Jefferson shrugged. "A bit agoraphobic maybe."

"Agoraphobic?" Afraid of going away from home? Was he actually a recluse? Maybe that would explain the closed door to the second bedroom and why she never saw him in the dining room.

Jefferson glanced at Nancy. "If you ask me, he hangs around that apartment all the time. He's not playing golf or going out of town. If that's not agoraphobia, what is?"

They strolled through the garden gate and waited for Louise to join them. She walked alongside back to the main building as she took off the gloves and helmet.

"How's the petition going?" asked Nancy.

"It's moving." Louise looked back at the garden and the hive beyond. "That hive is pretty healthy, so far, but that won't last long if they start using pesticides. I've got to get more names on my petition. I don't want to come out one morning and find the little critters all dead. Fortunately," she held up a finger and grinned. "I've enlisted the entire garden club here and the nature and conservation clubs are behind me, and they'll all be collecting signatures too." She nodded to herself. "I think we've got this one beat."

***

Garden Notes

> Sherry Palance, Chair of the Garden Committee, reminds all residents that no pesticides or herbicides are to be used in the community garden or in the

gardens around the terraces. Pests can be controlled by inspecting plants and removing injurious pests by hand or by using ladybugs, praying mantises and other beneficial insects. Weeding must be done by hand. These measures are necessary to protect our lovely environment and our honey bees, beneficial insects, and the diversity of bird life at Whisperwood. Thank you.

- *The Whisperwood Breeze, Newsletter for Whisperwood Retirement Village*

CHAPTER 17

The day for Betts' memorial service had arrived. By the time Nancy walked into the chapel, it was filling up. Sounds were hushed as people took their seats on pews facing the altar. A large stained glass window of a white dove on a blue ground lit up the wall behind the altar. No religious symbols graced the large room since the chapel was used by different religious denominations. Such symbols were portable and brought in as needed. Soft piano music added to the solemn feel pervading the sanctuary.

Nancy glanced at the front pew, usually reserved for the immediate family. African-Americans filled the entire row. A small boy twisted in his seat and peered at the audience over the back of the pew. Three teenagers, two older couples, and an elderly woman who could pass for a Whisperwood resident took up the rest of the pew and sat with heads bowed. Was the older woman Betts' sister? Grace also sat near the front. No Richard in evidence. Nancy saw her dab at her eyes with a handkerchief. Where was Samira?

Nancy scanned the rest of the chapel and spotted Samira almost hidden by a pillar in the back row. Ruth Smith also sat in the back row, leafing through a hymnal. Then Nancy noticed Louise, George, and Fitz sitting together in a central pew and waving to get her attention. She nodded and joined them.

"I don't see Jefferson and Helen here," whispered Louise.

Nancy surveyed the room. She didn't see them either, but she hadn't expected to. She was curious about Betts' family, though. She hoped this would be a service where the officiator would at least hint at who the deceased was. All too often in this chapel, the service was an impersonal recitation of Biblical quotes with only a passing mention of the deceased. Very unsatisfying to her, and she wasn't even family of the departed.

Louise leaned over to whisper to Nancy, "Buck up, it's going to be a Unitarian service. They brought the minister over from the Charlestown congregation. Betts was a long-time Unitarian and worked with them on social justice issues. You know, like civil rights, gay rights, marriage equality. Stuff like that. My kind of person. Wish I'd known her better."

"Me, too." Nancy relaxed. The service for Betts would be in good hands. Then she noticed that the person sitting up front facing them, no doubt the minister, was a woman. Even better.

The minister stood and walked to the pulpit. She wore a simple black dress and a stole of pale blue with the symbols of religions around the world. "Welcome," she said, "I am the Reverend Gail Stevens, and I am pleased to be the minister for this service in which we honor the memory of Elizabeth Theresa Horner, known to her friends and family as Betts." She paused to smile at the relatives in the front pew.

She invited a woman from the front row to come forward and light a large candle on the table in front of the lectern. The smell of candle wax wafted across the room. Then the minister came forward again and led the group in a hymn. Once that was done, she looked out at the audience, shifted her eyes to the front pew and smiled at the family.

"Betts Horner was a believer in justice," the minister began. Nancy leaned forward to hear better. She wanted to know who Betts Horner was.

"And she worked toward that end in every aspect of her life," the minister continued. Then she proceeded to describe Betts' upbringing in an African-American family in Virginia, family accounts of her feistiness, her long career in a succession of law enforcement and security agencies and as a volunteer for various non-profit agencies. "She was a fighter against oppression and a champion for justice. We honor her memory today."

The minister invited friends and family to share special memories of Betts. Nancy looked around to see who would respond as a soft murmur spread among those assembled there. A sixtyish woman in the front row rose and turned to face the assembly. She was slim with short-cut gray hair, and she wore a black pantsuit. A white blouse under her jacket peeked out at her throat.

"My name is Geri Horner. Betts was my older sister." The voice was soft but strong. The minister stepped down with a microphone in her hand and held it in front of the woman's face. She took the microphone. "Betts fought my battles for me all my life. And she fought for justice and freedom against oppression. Now I will have to fight her last battle." She paused to wipe a tear away. She took a deep breath and in a louder voice continued. "We will find the person who cut her life short." She paused again and deliberately focused on individuals around the room. "You can count on that." There was a stunned silence as she handed the microphone back to the minister.

"Uh, yes, well," the minister stammered. She held out the microphone. "Anyone else?"

No one wanted to follow Betts' sister, so the minister led the assembly in a hymn, then closing words and a benediction.

The sounds of a cheery postlude from the piano followed Nancy and the others into the anteroom for the brief reception. Coffee, lemonade, and cookies had been spread out on tables, all provided by Whisperwood as usual for memorial services. She thanked the minister and offered condolences to the family as she greeted them in the receiving line. As Nancy shook Geri's hand, she said softly, "Betts had a lot of friends here. We will find the murderer. I hope you'll come see me later," She looked meaningfully into Geri's eyes, which were every bit as shrewd as Betts' had been. Nancy wondered how Geri made her living.

Geri frowned at her. "You'll help? You're the detective, aren't you? Betts told me about you. Thank you for being on our side."

"Come see me if you need to talk. We can pool our information, work together," Nancy said. "I'm in Apartment 101. First floor, end of the hall past the dining room."

Geri nodded. "I'll come by later. I'd like to know what you know."

Nancy realized she was holding up the line. She moved on to greet other members of the family, then joined Louise and George who were sipping coffee as they hovered near the wall, listening to the comments around them. The receiving line was breaking up, and Betts' family, being outsiders, huddled together in the far corner. Seeing this, Nancy walked over to the family, telling them how much she had enjoyed knowing Betts. The younger children had taken to playing in the hall while the rest of the family eagerly accepted Nancy's remarks and added anecdotes of their own.

As Nancy walked back to her apartment, she reflected on the love and intelligence shown by the family. The older ones were all teachers or social workers. Betts had taken a different path. Nancy watched Geri work the crowd, praising Betts and her accomplishments. "She never talked about what she did," added Geri, "she let most people think she was ordinary folk, but she wasn't. Not at all." Nancy heard the love in Geri's voice but also saw that Geri listened with sharp glances then and there as others made comments.

Watching Geri engaged Nancy's attention and she became so absorbed in her thoughts that she passed without noticing the bleak-faced woman who crept along with one hand on the hall rail. Only later did Nancy realize that the woman was Alicia Perrygrew, who had stared so intently at her in the dining room. What great tragedy had left the woman so sad and shaken?

***

An hour later, Nancy heard a knock on the door, shooed Malone into the back room, and opened the door to Geri. "Samira's letting me stay with her in their apartment till I find out who did this," she said, as she followed Nancy into the living room. "They're not going to get away with it."

"Coffee? Tea?" Nancy asked as Geri contemplated the clutter of Nancy's living room. "Just push those magazines aside and sit on the couch."

"I don't need anything, thanks," said Geri, making a place to sit. "Except to talk. Have you found out anything that would help?"

Nancy thought of the undercurrents swirling around Jefferson and Helen Topham and Samira. All vague and not worth mentioning. "Not yet. Had Betts mentioned to you anything she suspected?" Nancy asked, taking a pile of magazines off the easy chair and sitting down to face Geri.

"Just that something bad is happening here." Geri gazed around Nancy's apartment. "She didn't say what, but she had suspicions." She pulled a flyer out of her purse. Nancy recognized it as an announcement for the upcoming lecture on consumer fraud. "I saw this. It's the kind of thing Betts knew about. I think she was killed because she found out what's going on here. She knew something was wrong. Something criminal."

A shadow crossed Nancy's soul, a feeling of deja vu. Isn't this what she and Louise and George said last year when they began questioning the accidental deaths and discovering the exploitation taking place at Whisperwood? Those culprits were dead or in prison, and everything had seemed to be going smoothly, but now scammers were targeting the people here. Or was it just that the elderly are targets and Whisperwood had the right demographic? Perhaps it was as simple as that.

"She was a nice person," said Nancy. "I didn't know her too well, and I am impressed by all that you had to say about her. She must have been strong."

Geri nodded. "She was that, but she was also civil and considerate." Geri choked on her words and groped blindly in her purse before bringing out a tissue and wiping her eyes with it. Then she leaned forward. "I also wondered if this could have been a racial attack," she said.

"Racial?" Nancy thought of Jefferson and Helen's bigoted comments. No doubt there were others, but a number of African-American and interracial couples lived at Whisperwood. She had not heard of other blatant racial attacks, but she'd ask Fitz later if he'd experienced any such thing. "I don't think so. Most of the people here are educated and kind, but I'll check around."

"Yeah. I'll see what my experience is like, living here for a couple of weeks." Geri smiled and winked at Nancy. "I'll be looking for any hints as to who might have killed her. I already checked her computer but didn't find anything relevant on it." She gazed at the window and tapped her chin. "Actually, I didn't find much on it at all. The history cache was cleared too."

She looked at Nancy. "Now you know that in the work she did, she used the computer a lot. And if she was onto something here, don't you think she would have logged onto some databases? Why would she clear the history cache? The computer was locked in her own apartment for her sole use."

Right. Why would she? Nancy knew that business about Betts' computer had been bothering her. "Samira said you'd erased the files before giving it to one of the kids in the family."

"She said that? I'm the only one in the family who's been in the apartment, clearing out Betts' stuff." Geri tapped her fingers on the chair arm, pushing her lips in and out as she thought. "Yeah, I did give all her electronics stuff—iPod, Kindle, and her computer—to the kids, but I checked everything first. The history cache was already cleared."

Nancy nodded. "So clearing the history cache erased a record of websites that Betts might have visited in tracking down possible criminals. Would be useful to know whose names she was searching, but that would make clearing the cache an important task for a criminal. Of course, that person had to enter Betts' apartment to do it." She paused. "Or it was Samira."

"Samira?" Geri stared down at her hands. "Samira. I suppose she could have done it. Hate to think it, they'd been so close at one time." She glanced at Nancy with a grin. "Till they started sharing that apartment."

"We will have to put her on the list as a suspect even though she was Betts' friend and roommate. Of course, Betts may have been in the habit of routinely clearing the history cache. That's probably what happened, but who else would have done it?" Nancy remembered Betts' shrewd glance at something Grace had said, as if Betts had deep and private thoughts on the subject. "She noticed things, didn't she? That might make some people uneasy."

"She did." Geri studied her hands. "But whatever she thought, she usually kept it to herself. Sometimes she let people think she was, well, a bit dumb, you know?"

A good attitude for finding out about people. "Have you talked to the sheriff?" asked Nancy.

"Of course. He was courteous to me and the family. No complaints yet," said Geri. "I guess he knows I'm just waiting to fault him on something, but mainly," she hesitated and gulped, "mainly, I hope he knows his job. Most of you are nice people. I'd hate for him to make a mistake."

"Me too, but he can use our help, whether he knows it or not," said Nancy. "We live here and know what's going on. He does not." She studied her fingernails. "He tends to patronize."

"You know it, girl." Geri laughed. She stood to leave. "So right now, we'll both be looking for racist activity from anyone here, and I'll keep going through Betts' papers and files for clues as to why someone would murder her. I'll feel Samira out as a suspect, but that's hard to imagine. Do you have any suggestions?"

Nancy thought before answering. "There's a couple here who insulted Betts and seemed to have some agenda that included her, but I'm just guessing about that. Jefferson and Helen Topham. Keep an eye out for anything that involves them."

Geri took a pen and notepad out of her purse and made a note. "Anything else?"

"I have some ideas of my own I'll be looking into," said Nancy. "Probably way off base but worth checking out. Just be careful. Everyone here knows you have to clean out her place and are probably looking through her files. They probably feel pretty confident that you won't find anything if they erased Betts' files. Keep them thinking that, or you might become a target too."

***

Shredder Day Is Coming!

The shredder truck will be at Whisperwood from 9 a.m. until 12 noon next Saturday morning. This is a safe and easy way to get rid of old documents and other papers you no longer need. Just bring them in a paper bag to the parking area. The bags will be taken from you and tossed into the shredder as you watch. No reservations needed.

- *The Whisperwood Breeze, Newsletter for Whisperwood Retirement Village*

CHAPTER 18

After Geri left, Nancy noticed the time. If she hurried, she could make the afternoon aerobics swimming class. Wearing a robe over her bathing suit, Nancy strode toward the swimming pool at the other end of the building. After the attack on her in the dressing rooms last year, she chose to swim in a class rather than alone, and she was going to be late for this one if she didn't hurry.

As Nancy passed Grace's apartment, the door opened and Grace stepped out. The blue overalls she wore over a flannel shirt emphasized her stoutness. A floppy sun hat covered her head. "Nancy! Just the person I wanted to see." She fell into step next to Nancy. "Have any ideas about the secret of that old clock yet?"

Nancy slowed her stride to match Grace's. "Nothing yet. I don't see anything that could be a code or cipher or any other kind of secret message." Nancy glanced at Grace's plain face, thinking of the inner strength needed to endure the loss of two husbands. She refused to consider Helen's malicious hint that Grace had anything to do with her second husband's death. Nancy hoped Richard was treating his wife well.

Grace was chuckling as she walked. "I looked all over that clock for a code. First thing I thought of. No place to hide anything either. I can't imagine what the secret can be. Jefferson thinks it has a clue to the hidden Confederate treasure." She winked at Nancy. "I pretend I don't know about that, and he thinks he's pulling the wool over my eyes, but it's why he wants the clock so badly."

"What?" Nancy stopped walking. "A hidden Confederate treasure? Why do people keep saying that? I thought they were just making it up."

"Oh sure," Grace waved her hand to dismiss the idea. "That story's been around a long time. Can't understand why anyone would still believe it after all these years, but that's Jefferson for you."

"What's the story?" asked Nancy, intrigued.

Grace laughed and gave Nancy a sideways glance. "Caught your interest? Maybe you'll go after the treasure now. Makes the clock more appealing, doesn't it?"

"At least it explains why someone thinks the clock hides the key to a puzzle." Nancy looked at Grace expectantly. "So what is the story?"

They were approaching the lobby. Grace stopped walking and turned to Nancy. "Okay. Here goes. Historians and treasure hunters have speculated about this, so you can't blame my family for thinking about it too.

"Seems that millions of dollars' worth of gold was lost or unaccounted for after the Civil War. Supposedly some of the Confederate treasury was hidden to wait for the South to rise again or," Grace grinned, "just to make sure the Union army didn't get it.

"One story has it that when the Union army was going to invade New Orleans, the Confederate soldiers carted millions of dollars worth of gold away from New Orleans to Columbus, Georgia, to hide it in a safer place. The gold was temporarily stored at William H. Young's Iron Bank." In October of 1862, a year after the war began, General Beauregard was ordered to take the gold from the bank." Grace smiled and winked at Nancy.

"You don't think the Young bank would give it up that easily, do you? Of course not, but the bank was forced to hand it over and then it just disappeared. Mystery ever since." Grace arched an eyebrow at Nancy. "Believe it or not."

Great story, Nancy thought. She loved hidden treasure legends. Was it true? She'd google it later, but it certainly might explain Jefferson's interest in the clock. "The clock was in Richmond during the Civil war. Why would it hide a clue to a treasure from Georgia?"

"Why not?" Grace shrugged. "That's my guess. Of course, a lot of people were hiding their valuables what with the invading armies coming through. Even my own family has a story like that. The clock might hide a clue to that or anyone else's hidden treasure, I guess."

"The clock is valuable as it is," said Nancy. "I looked it up on the Internet and a clock very much like it was on an auction site going for fifteen hundred dollars."

"Fifteen hundred dollars," Grace repeated thoughtfully. "Nice chunk of change."

"But not a secret," said Nancy, glancing at Grace. Surely she wouldn't sell a family heirloom. None of them seemed to need the money.

As they entered the lobby, Nancy waved at Louise who had been joined by three other women at the petition table. The front doors were propped open, letting in the warm spring breeze and the scent of new-mown grass.

Grace looked at Louise's set-up and snorted. "Ridiculous," she said under her breath, but Nancy heard her.

"Why?" asked Nancy, nodding toward Louise. "The loss of bees is a worldwide crisis."

Grace looked up, startled. "Why? It's just a hive of bees, for

Pete's sake. Let the landscaping crew do their job. It's nothing to do with us. If just one bee stings an allergic person, this place will be sued to high heaven." She glanced at her watch. "Got to run. See you later." She rushed out the front door toward the parking area without looking back.

Nancy gave Louise the "V" sign and hurried on to the swimming pool.

***

Later that afternoon, Nancy walked down the hall to Fitz's apartment and knocked on the door.

Fitz opened it with a yawn, coffee cup in hand. "Nancy! Come on in. Wondered where you've been keeping yourself."

"Been around," said Nancy with a smile as she stepped into Fitz's apartment. He had moved in months before, but the room still had all the charm of a warehouse. The TV set balanced on top of two boxes, other boxes lined the walls, and the couch and armchair still had drop cloths on them. Nancy sat on the couch drop cloth. "I was talking to Betts' sister Geri and she had some disturbing observations. I'd like to get your take on them, see what you think, if you don't mind."

"For you? Of course not, Luv." He sat in the armchair, crossed his legs, and smiled at her, his white teeth gleaming in the dark face. For once, he wasn't wearing a tool belt. "Fix yourself a cup of tea."

"I'm fine, thank you." Nancy smiled back at him. She had known Fitz for decades. When they'd first met so many years ago, he had carried a big chip on his shoulder—not surprising in those days of blatant discrimination and a separate but equal policy. Over the years, they had learned to like and trust each other, and Nancy was surprised and delighted to find that he had followed her to Whisperwood.

Now she sought a way to begin what might be an upsetting

conversation. She settled for the innocuous. "What did you think of Betts' memorial service?"

Fitz nodded. "Very nice. Pleasant family. Enjoyed meeting them."

"I did, too," said Nancy. "And Betts' sister Geri was quite forceful in her statement."

Fitz took a sip of coffee. "She was that, and she was talking to the right people about finding Betts' killer. Hey, we're part of the 90s Club, you know. We're hot on the trail of the culprit." He winked at her. "At least I hope you are."

"I wish," said Nancy. "Geri came over to my apartment afterwards, and we talked." Nancy hesitated, knowing this might be a sensitive subject for Fitz, but then she plowed ahead. "She's wondering if the murder was racially motivated." Nancy rushed on. "It's hard to believe such a thing would happen here at Whisperwood, but. . . ." She took a breath. "It's a possible clue to the killer."

Fitz rubbed his chin. "I see. And you wonder if I might have seen something like that here or been a victim myself. Probably you want a list of the bigots I might have met here."

Nancy nodded, hating to suggest such an ugly thing existed at Whisperwood.

He leaned back in the armchair. "I know you would like to think that racial hatred is an anomaly. . ."

Nancy started to protest, but Fitz held up his hand and studied her for a moment. He cleared his throat. "I'm going to tell you how I see it. We're friends, aren't we? This isn't easy." Fitz leaned back, waiting for her response.

"Of course. You can tell me what you think." The warmth of friendship and caring she felt for Fitz had grown over the years. She knew he felt the same toward her. Why was he so hesitant now?

"You'll hate to hear this, but you are privileged. You've always been privileged." He smiled as she sputtered a protest and continued. "White, upper middle class, educated. A good reputation, power, money, jobs—they're all handed to you." Fitz stopped to take a breath. "But for me, for Betts, even today, although it's better than in the past, we have to prove ourselves again and again. Just ask President Obama."

Nancy wanted to argue with him, but even as she tried to put together her case, she knew every word he said about her was true. The toughest battle she'd fought in her life was getting her private investigator license, but even the way to that had been smoothed by her father, his knowledge and his connections. She sighed. Fitz was right. All the result of white privilege.

Fitz leaned forward. "I never told you this. . ."

Nancy listened, chastened, and heard the sadness in his voice. She thought she had known Fitz well, but now she realized that he'd revealed little more than the surface. He sat in the comfortable old armchair and watched her as if expecting her to back away from him, as if only the surface of his soul was acceptable to her.

"What have you never told me?" she asked softly, looking directly at him. "I've always thought of you as one of my dearest friends. I want to know."

"Remember when we first met?" Fitz asked. "I was pretty bitter at the time. Not pleasant to be around." He paused to sip his coffee.

Nancy nodded and thought of Fitz as he had been so many years ago. She had pushed and pestered him to notice her in the face of his obvious aversion. The truth was, she hated to admit, that she was young and naive and had never met anyone so antagonistic. Most people liked her. She couldn't understand someone who so obviously did not.

"I had a son once," said Fitz. He smiled at her startled reaction. "I know, I never told you about him. Hurt too much. His name was

Adam, a sweet boy, very smart, like his mother. When he was ten, he was bicycling to school like he did every morning. But that morning someone in a pick-up truck drove by, yelling slurs at him and then. . ." He stopped, closed his eyes, and took a deep breath. "And then they shot and killed him."

"What? They shot your son?" Nancy sat horrified.

"There were witnesses, but somehow the cops never found the murderers." He paused, staring down at his shoes. After a moment, he continued.

"His mother and I. . . we could never get beyond that. She left me. I don't know where she is now. Don't care." He sighed and gazed at the wall behind Nancy. "All he was doing was bicycling down the road. Kids ought to be able to bicycle down a road."

Nancy listened, hoping her face showed sympathy and caring and not the horror and intense shock that vibrated through her body. How could she have known Fitz for so long and not known of this supreme tragedy in his life? Had his distrust of white people included her? It saddened her to think that his smiling, congenial exterior hid the truth of his feelings and this tragedy. Their easy friendship was surface only. She did not know Fitz at all.

The fact stunned her. She wanted to leave, but to leave would seem like rejection. She needed to be alone to reassess and, perhaps, atone for all the times she had exploited her white skin, blue eyes, blonde hair—not that she had done so deliberately, but she had gotten what she wanted not necessarily because of her ability.

Then she thought of the times she had let racist inferences pass because to object would bring denial and unpleasantness. She occasionally played bridge with one woman, in particular, who disguised her prejudice against the African-American staff at Whisperwood with patronizingly sweet comments. Once that woman had been annoyed enough to use the "N" word. Nancy remembered how she had covered her own shock at such ugly crudeness instead of confronting the woman. Much to atone for indeed.

Fitz interrupted her musings with a chuckle. "I can see I bothered you, but we're still friends, right?"

Nancy looked at him and nodded, although his comments had shocked and troubled her. She struggled to reply. "Don't keep such things about your life a secret from me, okay? I care about you."

"Water under the bridge," said Fitz, brushing her comment aside. "You're really wondering about Betts Horner, and I'll tell you this. She'd been trained as an undercover agent. I've seen her work."

***

Share Your Career Day

> Many of you have led fascinating lives and held exciting jobs. As our young dining room servers finish high school and many go on to college, they would like to hear about your careers as they consider their own. The Whisperwood Dining Room staff invite you to an afternoon tea on Thursday at 2 p.m. in the dining room for an enjoyable afternoon of sharing and learning. Thursday. 2 p.m. Dining Hall.
>
> \- *The Whisperwood Breeze, Newsletter for Whisperwood Retirement Village*

CHAPTER 19

Nancy felt deeply moved as she left Fitz's apartment. She could not bear to return to the confined space of her own unit, one she was able to buy from the benefits of white privilege. She needed to do some soul-searching. She turned left and walked down the hall and out of the lobby to the nature trail that wound through the thin strip of woods behind the building. She glanced over toward the landscaped shrubbery where Betts' body had been found, but she had been shot late at night, not in broad daylight. People were around.

The quiet serenity of the trees on this warm day soothed her troubled spirit. As she entered a clearing and gazed up at the puffs of cloud floating in a deep blue sky, the infinity of the universe lent perspective to the horror of Betts' murder and Fitz's story. He had kept a terrible secret, yet he had lived a full life despite the tragedy. She had never suspected he was anything more than a lifelong bachelor.

And she called herself a detective.

Secrets. Everyone seemed to have secrets. Fitz's story made Bill's seem trivial. Bill had had an affair and fathered a child. A child who lived and breathed and now wanted to learn more about the father who had never actually raised her. What kind of man did that make him? The thought bothered her. Had he deserted the mother or had they drifted apart? Why hadn't he done the honorable thing?

Bill had rejected his own child, while Fitz would never see his child again and felt the extreme loss of it. Now Nancy had the opportunity to reclaim a life that Bill had apparently tossed away, leaving both of them bereft. She had had no children, but her life had been so full she had not felt the loss except for those rare moments when loneliness overwhelmed her. Perhaps, after all, she would leave a daughter, even if this daughter was an adopted one with parents of her own.

Whatever Bill had done was no longer relevant or important. What was important was the need to know and support a young life who had sought her out. To Nancy, who had outlived most of her family, this new insight lightened the load that had burdened her spirits since she had received the letter.

She took a bench at the turn of the trail and sat in the shade, imagining what this young girl might be like. How would they relate? Would they become friends? A warm breeze ruffled the leaves and the shrubs rustled. Twigs cracked as squirrels ran up and down trees. A cardinal trilled from a low shrub at the edge of the woods and a robin whinnied as it flew into the trees. Peace surrounded Nancy until she heard a sob. Shaken out of her own reverie, she peered down the path at the bowed figure walking her way. As the woman came closer, Nancy recognized Alicia Perrygrew. At last she might find out what had befallen that tragic figure.

Nancy patted the place next to her on the bench. "Won't you join me?" she asked.

The woman looked up, tears streaking her face. "Ms. Dickenson, isn't it?" she said in a low, faltering voice.

"Call me Nancy. It's lovely sitting here in the quiet."

Nancy made her smile as welcoming as she could. What terrible thing could have happened to Alicia?

"Thank you." The woman sat with a sigh. She closed her eyes as if to feel the breezes better. Then she turned to study Nancy. "You're that private detective who saved Whisperwood last year."

"Not just me," Nancy corrected gently. Repeating this was getting quite tiresome. "The 90s Club did that."

"But you're part of that," Alicia said. "We haven't met. I'm Alicia Perrygrew."

Nancy extended her hand. "Nice to meet you."

"I wonder if you can help me," Alicia whispered, more to herself than to Nancy. She frowned down at the pebble-strewn path.

Nancy was quick to follow this opening. "I'll certainly be glad to try. What's the problem?"

"I am so troubled," Alicia began. Her eyes teared up. "You'll think me such a fool."

"I've made a fool of myself so many times, I don't even count them any more." Nancy said. She put an arm around Alicia and hugged her. "Anyway, I've heard it all."

She was curious, but more than that, she was concerned. In Nancy's experience, sharing sadness and worry was a step toward healing and moving beyond the trouble. But she didn't want to risk scaring Alicia away, so she didn't push.

"It started so. . .so innocently," Alicia said. "I had no intentions of following through on anything. I was just curious, you see." She glanced at Nancy as if to gauge her reaction. "And a bit lonely."

"I see," murmured Nancy. "I do all kinds of crazy things out of curiosity."

Alicia smiled tentatively. "I just thought I'd see, you know. It was harmless, I thought." Alicia pulled out a tissue and blew her nose. "I went to one of those online dating sites, and. . ." she wiped her eyes, "and I filled out one of their forms." She peeked at Nancy out of the corner of her eye as if seeking censure or a reprimand. Nancy kept her face pleasantly noncommittal.

Alicia continued. "I didn't think anyone would date someone my age, so I fudged a little bit, and I put in someone else's photo. Like I said, I had no intention of following through with anything."

"A lot of people do that," Nancy said reassuringly. She suspected where this was going. She knew the daughters of friends who had met men through the Internet. One of them even married the man. Not a happy match, as it turned out.

"Then I got a response from a gentleman." She looked at Nancy. "He seemed to be a very nice man."

"I get it. A very nice man," repeated Nancy.

"Oh he was." Alicia looked inward. "At least I thought he was. And we liked all the same things. So we started e-mailing each other." She took out another tissue and twisted it in her hands. "There was no harm in it. I knew that as soon as he found out how old I was, that would be the end of it. Still, it was so nice to get his e-mails and to share my thoughts with him."

"And then," Nancy said, "Things became more serious. He told you he loved you."

Alicia turned to Nancy. "How did you know?"

Nancy shook her head. "And then he needed to borrow some money."

"He did, but Nancy," Alicia laid a hand on Nancy's arm, "it wasn't what you think."

Nancy swallowed her skepticism and refrained from heaving a sigh or raising an eyebrow. Alicia didn't need that. "Tell me what happened next," Nancy said gently.

"He was living overseas for his company, and his daughter became very ill over here. He couldn't cash a check there so he could buy an airline ticket to come home." Alicia looked at Nancy. "You know how it is in some of those countries. Hard to get cash when you need it."

"That's what he told you, I guess," said Nancy.

"Oh, but I'm sure it was true." Alicia declared. "Why would he lie to me? We were in love. I know he loved me." At that, Alicia burst into tears. "Impossible, I know," she said through her sobs. "Once we met, it would be over."

Nancy put her arm around Alicia as she sobbed. "How much did you send him?"

Alicia forced herself to stop crying and dabbed at her eyes with the tissue. "I am so ashamed." She blew her nose. "I wired him ten thousand dollars, and. . ." she drew a deep breath, "I haven't heard from him since." She began sobbing again.

Nancy let her cry. Ten thousand dollars was the usual take from such scammers. After the sobs diminished, Nancy asked her, "Are you all right financially now? You have other funds?"

Alicia sat up. "I don't understand why he hasn't e-mailed me. He said he loved me and wanted to be with me. He wanted to get together when he returned to see his daughter."

She looked at Nancy and blushed. "Of course, I couldn't let that happen. As soon as he saw me, he'd realize what I'd done, but it was so nice." She brushed a tissue across her eyes. "It was just so nice. . ." She shook her head. "I've been alone ever since my husband died. Almost six years ago. That's a long time to be alone."

She stared out at the woods lost in her thoughts, then she heaved a huge sigh. "Thanks for letting me cry it out." After awhile she added, "I'll never see that money again, will I?"

Nancy shook her head.

"And I'll never hear from him either." Alicia's voice was sad, yet resigned. She sighed. "I guess I had it coming."

"He was a crook who took advantage of you," said Nancy.

"You're not the first and you won't be the last to be fooled. You did nothing wrong."

"That ten thousand dollars was my savings for a trip to Europe." She looked at Nancy with a tentative smile. "Guess I won't be going."

"You can file a report with the FBI, but you won't get your money back."

Alicia nodded. She rose, her face blotched with tears but it didn't seem as bleak. "Thank you, Nancy. I'm sorry I imposed on you like this, but you really helped."

"You'll be all right now, won't you?" asked Nancy.

"I think so." Alicia smiled. "I may not be able to go to Europe for a couple of years, but maybe I'll take the Whisperwood bus to the casino in Charles Town." She laughed. "Who knows? Maybe I'll win back my ten thousand dollars."

Nancy waved good-bye to her. From an Internet scammer to a casino. Seemed like Alicia was determined to lose her money. Nancy made a mental note to invite Alicia to lunch and to seek her out in the future.

No one else ventured by as Nancy continued to sit on the bench. The warm breezes, droning insects, and scents of flowers made her feel drowsy, and she dozed there for several minutes. Finally, she took the trail back to the main building, then walked behind it over to the garden. As she hoped, Louise stood in bee suit, hat, and gloves working her hive. She was just replacing the hive cover as Nancy approached..

"Are you finished?" Nancy called out.

Louise looked up and waved. "Yep. Let me pick up my tools and I'll go back with you."

Nancy waited as Louise placed the tools into the backpack and slipped her arms through the straps. She grabbed her cane, and they walked to the main building together.

"What's happening?" Louise asked.

A fleeting memory of Alicia crossed her mind, but Nancy smiled, pleased at the resolution she had made in her own life about the letter. "I'm going to invite Bill's daughter to visit me. I've thought about it, and I admit her letter was a bit of a shock, but now I think I'd like to meet her."

Louise stopped walking. She squinted at Nancy in the bright sunlight. "Are you sure you want to do that?"

Good. Nancy had wanted Louise to play devil's advocate. Was her decision to get to know Bill's daughter a foolhardy one? What did Louise think? "Yes. I do," Nancy said and waited for Louise's response.

Louise walked along, chewing her lip as she stared down at the sidewalk. "The rather awkward circumstances of her birth," Louise began, "must make it difficult for you to accept her. No one would blame you for refusing her."

Nancy nodded. "Probably, but I wouldn't feel good about that, not that I'm happy about the whole circumstance, but she is not to blame. She may be the only relative I have left. I feel obligated to help. I could be good to her, and she could be good for me." She frowned. "Maybe. I hope so."

Louise hiked up the backpack of tools she carried. "Kind of hard managing a bee hive by yourself. Heavy work, actually." She stopped a moment to lean on her cane and catch her breath.

Nancy slowed her pace to match Louise's hobble as they walked along. Louise pushed her lips in and out as if she was thinking hard and finally said, "What if she wants something from you? What if she's just after your money?"

Like Alicia's e-mail buddy. Nancy nodded. "I've thought about that. She could be looking for a handout, I guess."

"She certainly could. Did you check her out using your detective know-how?" Louise asked. "Any criminal record?"

"The letter was such a shock. . ." Louise was right. Some kind of background check on this person should be undertaken before she set up any date to meet.

Louise cast Nancy a sideways glance. "Anyway, she might be connected to the scam artists preying on Whisperwood's residents. Wouldn't surprise me if she were."

Nancy stopped at the entrance. "That would be a coincidence."

"Not too much of one if she is a con artist," Louise said as the glass doors opened.

They walked across the lobby. At the elevator, Louise took Nancy's hand and squeezed it. "I know this has hit you hard. Just be careful. That's all I'm saying." She pressed the "Up" button. "See you at dinner." She looked at Nancy's sad face and added, "Unless you want me to stay with you a little while and talk."

Nancy roused herself. "I'm okay, but you're right about the background check." She gave Louise a quick hug, stepped back as the elevator doors opened and Louise entered, waving at Nancy as the elevator doors closed. Nancy strolled thoughtfully down the hall to her own apartment.

The first thing she saw when she opened the door was the letter. She had removed it from its hiding place in the desk and again propped it up on the table, but Malone needed her attention first. She spent a few minutes petting and talking to him. He rubbed himself against her leg, purring. Sometimes he was such a comfort. She gave him a treat, picked up the letter, and took it to her computer. She connected to the Internet and began a search on Ariana Van Allan, student at the University of West Virginia, Morgantown.

***

Support Our Students:
Fundraiser Picnic Planned for May

Whisperwood has a long history of providing scholarships, stipends, and internships to its student staff who serve you so well in the dining room. Twenty of our students head for college this fall. Plan now to attend the fundraising picnic to increase the scholarship funds available. Tickets are $25/person. All the picnic fixings, refreshments, games, and entertainment will be provided. Don't miss this exciting and worthwhile event. Pick up a flyer and buy your tickets at the reception desk in the lobby. You'll be investing in the future.

-The Whisperwood Breeze, Newsletter for Whisperwood Retirement Village

CHAPTER 20

"Just two weeks to go until they start spraying around here," called out Louise, pushing her petition and pen at a man ambling in from outside.

"What's this all about?" he asked, doffing the cowboy hat he wore. His face was craggy and tanned to leather.

Louise explained the cause of the honeybees as the man folded his arms, pursing his lips in and out and nodding as he listened.

"Good. You got it right," he said. "I'm the state apiarist, and I can tell you we bee people are mighty concerned about the state of the honeybees worldwide."

Nancy looked up to see Louise drop the clipboard in excitement. "State apiarist! You've got to look at my hive. It's out back. Only take a minute." Louise grabbed the man's arm. Then she stopped. "Oh wait. Don't have my bee suit here. How much time do you have?"

"Tight schedule. Just stopped by to visit my Grandma, then I have to hightail it back to Charleston."

"Oh, well, then." Louise stared at the floor, disappointment written on her face. "Maybe next time."

"Sure. Next time." He bent down, picked up the clipboard, and read the petition. "You make good points here," he said, handing the clipboard back to Louise. "Allowing for diversity of native plants in the landscape means you don't have to spray pesticides willy-nilly and, most times, shouldn't have to waste water on the landscaping either." He glanced out the wide glass doors of the entrance. "Save money for a place as big as this."

He nodded at her as he strode toward the elevator. "Keep up the good work!"

Louise walked over to Nancy and plopped down in the chair next to her. "I just met the state apiarist!"

Nancy smiled. "Congratulations."

Louise glanced at her and laughed. "I can see you're as thrilled as I am. However," she paused, "you will be excited to know that someone from the Attorney General's Office on consumer fraud will be speaking here next week. Just enough time to get the word out."

Nancy sat up. "That's wonderful. I'll put up posters announcing the talk. Just give me the particulars."

"Will do. Everyone should attend, so I'm planning two sessions for next Wednesday. Ten a.m. and two p.m."

"The auditorium holds about four hundred, which should be fine. We can try for everyone, but you know how that goes."

Louise groaned. "Sure. No matter how hard you plan, somebody gets sick, or decides not to come, or has friends visiting or whatever."

"This reminds me," Nancy closed her book, "of that flyer slipped under my door." She opened her purse and pulled it out.

Louise glanced at it. "I knew there were some dotty people living here, but whoever made that flyer wins the prize. Protect privacy? Privacy of what? Privacy to be swindled and duped? Protect privacy so swindlers can keep up their scams?"

"And it's anonymous," added Nancy. "Probably the scammers themselves wrote it. What would anyone else hope to gain?"

Louise shook her head. "They can't believe we'd be stopped by this bit of drivel."

"It is proof that the scammers live here," said Nancy, rereading the flyer. "To their advantage to cancel the talk."

Louise folded her arms stretched out her legs. "Keep the people here ignorant."

"And that way they'd still be potential victims, like cattle corralled in a stockyard." Nancy glanced at Louise.

Louise nodded. "Exactly." She sat up and stretched. "But what a stupid thing to do. Who'd fall for such an obvious ploy? The people here can't be that stupid."

Oh yes they can, Nancy wanted to say. Just amazing what people would buy into. She'd spent her career as a private detective being surprised at the swindles that succeeded. All the scammer needed was to fabricate a rush and the need for immediate action, fog the swindle with a lot of verbal decoration and mix in the victim's greed. She thought of Alicia. Playing the "I love you" card was the lowest blow of all and a powerful tool of abusers and predators alike.

"So how do we counter this?" Nancy said instead.

"Ignore it," said Louise. "But listen for the same sentiments among the residents. Someone might try to stir people up. They'd be sneaky about it but whoever it is has got to be linked to the scams going on here."

Nancy nodded. "Good plan. We'll have to alert Fitz and George too."

"And we'll all have to mix in with other groups to hear what's going on around the building."

Nancy watched the front doors open. Several women walked in

with shopping bags. "The shuttle's back from town," Louise muttered. She glanced at Nancy. "They've already signed." She waved at the women as they passed.

Louise hesitated before adding, "By the way, have you learned anything about your new relation?"

"Yes I have." Nancy smiled. "All good, no bad. She is a student at West Virginia University, her mother is a nurse, and, thank goodness, I didn't find any family with a criminal record. Actually, just a healthy, well-adjusted, middle class American family."

Louise applauded. "Terrific. Good thing you checked, but I'm glad that part is okay. Of course, that doesn't mean she's not after your money, but so far so good. How do you feel about her now?"

Nancy sighed. "I don't know yet. Suddenly I've become a stepmother with a newly acquired grown stepdaughter."

Nancy reflected on the circumstances. The young woman had been born before Nancy had met Bill, when he was in another time and place. A sad time, when he was facing the loss of his wife. What he had done in that painful time of loss may have provided the strength he needed to endure it, but it had nothing to do with her or her relationship with Bill. She always tried to do the kindest thing and the kindest thing would be to accept her new stepdaughter with love. She looked at Louise. "I'm getting used to it."

***

That evening at dinner, Nancy passed the flyer around the table for comment. She hadn't seen Fitz since their talk, and Nancy felt shy and hesitant around him. How did he feel now that he had revealed so much about himself? Did he feel as awkward as she did? She greeted him as usual. Nothing seemed amiss and he wore his usual outfit, including tool belt. She squeezed his arm and risked a glance at him. He saw it and for a moment his face went blank, then he winked at her. Nancy felt the tension ease from her shoulders.

He had shared bitter memories with her, and a lot had changed between them and yet nothing had changed. She smiled at him. Did he know how much she cared about him?

For a moment she had forgotten where she was, but then George whistled and she saw him pass the flyer on to Fitz. He scanned it and raised an eyebrow. "Trying to muddy the pond," he said.

"But have you heard any comments from the residents suggesting we not hold such a program?" asked Nancy.

"Not at all," Fitz said immediately.

George pushed his lips in and out. "Someone in the men's bridge club asked me if we were still holding the program in spite of the opposition. Had no idea why he thought anybody would object, but he said something about privacy. I thought he was kidding."

"After I talked to you, Nancy," said Louise, "my neighbor asked me if they were going to have to reveal their own mistakes with scammers. I told her of course not, but she had been listening to someone who is spreading rumors." Louise took a roll and spread butter on it. "Reminds me of the time when the Equal Rights Amendment for women didn't pass. You know why, don't you?"

"Absolutely ridiculous that it failed," said Nancy. "This day and age."

"I supported it," said George. "Can't imagine why it failed."

"I'll tell you why," said Louise, her eyes sparking. "Because the damn fools believed the rumors spread by its opponents that if it passed everyone would have to use the same bathrooms. That, my friends, was why it failed. Gullible fools. No telling what people might believe. So I think we should pay attention to that flyer and be ready to snuff out the stupidity and manipulation and remind the residents of the price of ignorance."

"Hear, hear," said George, lifting his wine glass to Louise.

Fitz and Nancy lifted their glasses as well, but Fitz set his down and frowned at them. "You realize, don't you, what this means?"

They looked at him.

"It confirms what we've been thinking. Someone who lives here has an interest in perpetuating the scams that victimize our friends and neighbors. That flyer was a stupid attempt to stop you, Nancy, since it was delivered to you and not to the rest of us, from investigating further. What will the scammer do next?"

"Those three attempts on your life make sense now," grumbled George.

"Don't eat any candy delivered anonymously to your door," muttered Louise.

"I think we'll all have to be careful from now on," added Fitz.

***

Reminder: Local Stores Will Deliver

> Whisperwood provides a real boost to the local economy by providing jobs for the community and customers for its locally grown and produced vegetables, arts, crafts, pizza and other items. Shuttles make frequent runs into town for your convenience, but most shops and merchants in town will deliver your order to Whisperwood. A list of merchants who will deliver is available at the reception desk.
>
> - *The Whisperwood Breeze, Newsletter for Whisperwood Retirement Village.*

CHAPTER 21

Nancy woke to the sound of Malone growling out the bedroom window as he sat on the windowsill. His tail flicked back and forth in rhythm with the red lights that flashed through her window and onto the walls. She rushed to the window.

Two fire trucks had pulled up to the front entrance. From the shouts and the running firefighters, Nancy gathered that there was a fire at Whisperwood.

She threw on some clothes and whispered a few soothing words to Malone as she coaxed him into his crate so he'd be secure in case they had to get out of the building. Then she rushed to the hall door. Just before she opened it, she touched the doorknob, then gripped it. It was cool, and no smoke was leaking in under the door. She cracked the door and peered out. No fire. No flame. She walked down the hall, joining other residents, all on her side of the hall, looking toward the front of the building.

"What's going on?" asked one, then another, as they hurried toward the lobby.

A heavyset man in firefighter's uniform barred them from entering the lobby. Nancy could see the hoses stretched across the lobby floor from the truck to the auditorium. She smelled smoke and burning wood, fabric, and probably plastic, but soon the stench of burning materials turned to the tang of wet ash. Nancy guessed the fire was out, but what was the damage?

Harry Doyle came running toward them, then pushed his way through the onlookers to speak to a firefighter standing on the sidelines. The firefighter took Harry into the auditorium. A few minutes later, Harry emerged, shaking his head. He disappeared into his office.

One of the firefighters ambled toward them. "All right, folks," he said. "Show's over. You can go home now."

Nancy turned to join the others grumbling to each other as they returned to their apartments. Nancy's mind picked through the implications. Someone had set a fire in the auditorium. Why? To prevent a talk by someone from the Attorney General's Office? What a ridiculous thing to do. At the worst, the fire might delay the talk until the auditorium was back to normal. Was the auditorium scheduled for any other controversial activity that might provoke such sabotage?

Nancy realized she was assuming arson, but perhaps it was an accident. She turned around and went back to the lobby. She watched them stretch tape across the auditorium door. Did that mean they considered it arson?

A quick glance toward Harry's office and she could see a light on. Harry must be contacting the insurance company now.

She watched the hoses retreat, then the remaining firefighters cleared the area, boarded the trucks and headed out and down the mountain toward town. Nancy walked over to Harry's office and knocked. She heard a brisk "Come in" and opened the door.

Harry was on the phone. He looked up and gestured for her to enter. His eyes were bleary, and he wore pajama tops over black slacks with no socks.

Nancy sat in the visitor's chair and waited while Harry made arrangements for an insurance investigator to inspect the damage.

He hung up and spit out the word. “Arson.”

“Unbelievable,” said Nancy.

“Yes.” He ran his hands over his head. “Like I need this.”

“Did a security guard discover it? Why didn’t he sound the alarm for the residents to get out of the building?

“He said it was contained to a small area of the auditorium. He called for back-up and the fire department, then tried to put it out with an extinguisher. By that time it had spread to the furnishings and the fire department had arrived. They were quick, I’ll say that for them.”

“Still we need a better procedure to protect the residents.”

Harry nodded. “I’ll check into that tomorrow.”

Nancy rested her chin in her hand. “Why would anyone want to set fire to the auditorium?”

Harry picked up a pencil and snapped it in two. “I have no idea,” he said through gritted teeth.

“Are there any bookings that might be controversial?”

“The Baptist Church choir was scheduled for next Tuesday evening, and then, of course, the speaker from the Attorney General’s Office on Wednesday. Nothing controversial at all.” Harry leaned back in his chair, pushing his lips in and out. “I can’t believe this.”

“Neither can I,” said Nancy, “but until the auditorium is repaired, we can use the dining room.”

Harry snapped his fingers. “Great idea, Nancy.” His face brightened. We’ll just make the concert a little later, after the dinner crowd has left, and the speaker from the AGO can give her lecture in midmorning and mid-afternoon as we planned. That won’t inconvenience the lunch crowd at all.”

“Did they say how the fire started? I thought the auditorium was locked up when it wasn't in use."

Harry nodded. "It's certainly supposed to be, but the cleaning crew has taken to leaving doors to the auditorium and the basement classrooms unlocked. Makes it easier not having to transfer keys from one person to the next." His eyes narrowed. "That will have to change."

"I'm sorry this happened," Nancy said. "You're doing a great job as administrator, even with the crises we keep having around here." She rose and stepped to the door.

Harry followed her. "Thank you." He pulled out a key and locked the door to his office. "I always lock it," he said.

When Nancy returned to her apartment, Malone greeted her from his crate with anxious meows. She released him and petted him with soothing words. The phone rang.

"What's going on down there?" Louise. "Are you all right?"

"I'm fine," said Nancy, "but the auditorium was set on fire. Arson."

"Arson!" Louise shrieked. "The auditorium?"

"Yes."

Louise didn't speak for a moment. Nancy waited.

"You know what this means," Louise said at last.

"Final confirmation. The scammer lives or works here," said Nancy.

"Yes," said Louise. "And they are stepping up their efforts to prevent us from stopping their lucrative lifestyle. Whoever it is knows who we are and where we live. We're all in danger."

***

Emergency Rules

We regret to inform you that because of a fire in the auditorium, all activities planned for that venue will either be postponed or held in the dining room. Signs will be posted to alert you to the changes. This will be a good time to review your own safety precautions. In case of emergency, staff will assist and escort those who require assistance out of the building. Be sure you know the closest exit out of the building from your apartment and from any of the classrooms and other facilities on the campus.

-Posted on the Whisperwood Notice Board

CHAPTER 22

The next Wednesday, the dining room was packed with only standing room left against the walls fifteen minutes before ten when the first presentation on consumer fraud would begin. Word had spread throughout the building that an arsonist had attempted to stop the presentation, and now most residents were curious to hear what the fuss was all about.

Nancy leaned against the wall at the side. If the auditorium arsonist had hoped to cancel or delay the day's presentation, he had to be sorely disappointed. The dining room staff had set up a coffee and tea station in the back and were offering a spread of pastries and fruit. This would not have happened in the auditorium.

Louise walked over to stand next to Nancy. "Couldn't have asked for a better turnout," she said, coffee cup in hand.

"That should please the arsonist," Nancy muttered as she nodded in agreement. "Harry called the insurance company, and they're sending an investigator."

Louise looked around. "Can't get any more in the dining room. It has to be at capacity. Too crowded for my taste."

They watched Harry Doyle walk to the front of the room and tap on the microphone for attention. Unusual for him, Harry wore a suit and tie for the occasion. Conversation ceased, and the dining room became silent except for the inevitable coughs here and there..

"Thank you all for coming," he began. "Also thank you to the dining room staff for accommodating this impromptu change." He paused for the mild applause.

"I'm pleased to introduce today's speaker, Ms. Catherine Albright, from the West Virginia Office of Consumer Fraud Investigations."

As Harry gave a brief biography of the speaker, Nancy studied the athletic-looking woman sitting on stage behind him. She wore a teal pantsuit and tailored white blouse with gold earrings and necklace. She kept a frozen smile on her face, but as she scanned the audience, she noticed Nancy's intent expression and winked at her. Nancy nodded and smiled back. They had met before at a conference on crime in Charleston. Nancy was surprised Catherine had recognized her.

Harry finished his introduction and Catherine approached the microphone.

"Thank you, Mr. Doyle. I'm very pleased to be here." She smiled a welcome to the crowd and raised a hand. "How many of you have received a scam offer of any kind?"

A flurry of hands rose. She nodded. "Most of you have, I see. If you spend any time on the Internet or if you have a land line, you assuredly have. Looking around the room here, you can all see how prevalent these scams are. Sadly, you are in the age group targeted by scammers. They see you as having a high disposable income and time on your hands. You're inclined to be polite and will listen to their pitch instead of hanging up on them."

Catherine waited as the audience joked, grumbled, or commented on her words. "So. . .I'm hereby giving you permission to hang up on anyone who wants your money for any reason. Okay?"

Someone yelled out "Amen" along with the laughter and scattered applause across the dining room.

Catherine nodded. "So here's what most scams have in common. Someone calls, texts, e-mails, or visits you claiming to be from the government, an established business, or a well-known charitable organization." Nancy watched the heads nod.

"By the way, don't trust caller ID. Scammers have technology that lets them display any number or organization on your ID screen." She paused and let her glance rest on various members of the audience before continuing.

"Here are some other ways they try to get your money. They'll send you an offer that sounds too good to be true. Maybe they'll say you've won a sweepstakes you don't remember entering and then they'll urge you to act immediately.

"Or they'll threaten you with arrest because of some fictitious unpaid bill or fine and insist you pay up within a couple of days. They always push for immediate or quick action. They don't want to give you time to think about it." She paused again for a moment as heads nodded across the room.

"Do not provide any financial, credit, or personal information unless you know that person is legitimate and has a legitimate reason for asking for the information. Same with wiring money or sending a pre-paid debit card. Once sent, it's almost impossible to reverse or trace the payment."

Nancy watched the audience. The dining room could not be darkened like the auditorium, so the room was light enough to read facial expressions. She watched for signs of distress or recognition as she scanned the audience. Many in the audience nodded their heads; a few whispered excitedly to their neighbors. She heard a gasp or two.

The speaker continued. "No agency of the government will call or e-mail you unless you initiate a call, e-mail or letter first. They may call to respond to your request. A government agency will also not ask for credit card or personal information by phone or e-mail.

"Insist on written documentation from anyone who claims you owe a debt. You can be sued for not paying a debt, but you cannot be arrested. Also request information in writing before donating money to a charitable organization. Do not provide credit card information over the phone to someone you don't know.

"And here's another scam. Someone sends you a check and asks you for money back. It takes weeks before you learn the check is no good. Don't send money or goods until your bank confirms that the check has been paid by the other bank."

She paused to take a sip of water before continuing. "All of this information is available in pamphlets through my office and online. I have copies on the tables at the front of the room. Pick one up as you leave." She shuffled her notes and looked out at the audience with a smile. "Now I'm sure you have questions."

Two men with hand mikes stood in the aisles to assist with questions. As Nancy listened, she noted the questions asked and, when she knew the questioner, the person's name. The program finally came to a close. Catherine thanked the audience, and Harry Doyle again took the microphone.

"As many of you know, we are conducting a survey on the scamming attempts that have been made on our residents. Copies of the survey are available at the reception desk in the lobby, so if you haven't filled one out yet, we would appreciate your doing so today. You do not have to sign the survey, so your privacy will be maintained." He turned to nod at the speaker. "Thank you, Ms. Albright, for your excellent presentation." He looked out at the audience. "Let's all put our hands together in a big round of applause for Ms. Albright."

As the applause diminished, Louise walked across the front of the room, shook the speaker's hand and also thanked her for the talk. Louise then took the microphone and addressed the assembly. "I'd like to add to what Harry said about the survey. Even the smartest of us can be taken in by scammers who are clever, ruthless, and may be connected to organized crime. We know that many of you have received and even been victimized by the scams Ms. Albright talked about and perhaps others. We'd like to see if there is any pattern to the scams we get here." She paused as her words penetrated.

"You all know Nancy Dickenson, George Burrows, and Fitzhugh Connelly." She pointed to the side of the room where Nancy, George, and Fitz were standing. They raised their hands as heads turned their way.

"They will be at tables in the lobby after this talk and tomorrow morning. If you haven't filled out a survey form on this concern yet, please stop by the tables to let them know if you've received threatening phone calls, calls requesting money purporting to be from relatives or friends, or any other fraudulent claims requiring you to send money. You heard Ms. Albright's talk. Those are the scams I'm talking about. You'd help all of us by giving the information to me, Nancy, George, or Fitz. Thank you. You are free to return the forms anonymously if you are concerned about privacy." She turned to leave but then again grabbed the microphone. "And if you haven't signed the petition against chemical sprays on the landscaping, see me in the lobby. You can help protect our honeybees and our food and water supply."

Louise moved to the side as people picked up their belongings and slowly pushed the crowd along to follow Nancy, George and Fitz out the doors.

"Trust Louise to put in a plug for her project," George said.

Fitz took Nancy's arm and whispered in her ear, "Did you hear

Harry's comment about privacy? Someone got to him too."

The three took their places behind a long table, picked up their pens and smiled at their first customers. It looked like the lines were going to be long. Even if the residents had already turned in survey forms or were one of the lucky few who'd never been scammed, they all wanted to know what kind of information had been collected so far.

"We're still gathering the data," Louise told them.

***

Protect Yourself in Case of Fire

Whisperwood is designed to be safe and secure for all residents. Every Whisperwood apartment has smoke alarms, fire extinguisher, and a sprinkler system in case of fire.

Plan now to attend one of the upcoming training sessions on what to do in case of fire. Dates to be announced.

Know where the nearest exit is wherever you are in the building.

- *Posted Notice, Whisperwood Retirement Village*

Chapter 23

Late that afternoon, the 90s Club gathered in Nancy's apartment. Louise had cleared the clutter off the dining room table and wiped it clean of dust. Nancy made a pot of tea, and they all sat around the table while Malone snarled and hissed as he swatted at their shoes. Louise once put her hand down to pet him, but withdrew it just ahead of his swat. "Nothing much pleases him, I guess," she said to Nancy.

Nancy agreed. "Not much."

Fitz took the cup of tea from Nancy and sniffed it. "You're sure no one has been in your apartment but you?"

"Not that I know of," Nancy said, surprised. "Why?"

"Because it would be in the best interests of someone here for all of us to disappear." Fitz sipped the tea. "Add rat poison to the sugar, cyanide to the salt. That flyer, ineffective as it was, was a warning."

Louise looked up from scrutinizing a form. "Nancy's cheated death three times so far, and the auditorium was set on fire. The flyer is just milk toast."

"Milk toast?" George laughed. "Sorry. I know you're serious. Thank goodness Nancy escaped. She draws the heat away from the rest of us. Hard to think of myself as being dangerous to anybody." He scrunched his nose, bared his teeth, and narrowed his eyes. "I'll try, though."

"We all are dangerous to someone." Fitz picked up the pile of survey forms. "Setting fire to the auditorium shows how far they're willing to go." He waved the forms. "I was surprised at how many people filled these forms in. So how are we going to proceed? " He nodded at the sheaf of papers in his hand. "Lot of data there."

'So many of us have been targeted for scams here," said Nancy, "Do other retirement facilities have such a high rate of scam attempts?"

"I wondered about that, too," said Louise. She flicked her braid. "Sure looks as if someone here is supplying information about us to the scam artists." She took the pile of forms from Fitz and measured it with her fingers. "About an inch thick. We'll probably get more tomorrow, and we already have a bunch of responses from our earlier, more informal survey. We need to put all this in a database."

George sat up with interest. "I can do that. I'll take the forms back to my apartment and input the data on my computer. Nothing to it. Then we'll do a couple of sorts and see what we come up with." He turned to Nancy. "Should have told me that's what you were going for. Could have taken all those papers back to my apartment in the first place."

"All right, George." Nancy glanced through the surveys she held. "You're right. But since we're all here, I'd like to pick your brains on another subject. Does anyone have any ideas about Betts' death? Heard anything? Seen the sheriff do anything?"

Fitz stopped shuffling through the surveys and looked up. "The sheriff's been interviewing the people on her hall." He studied his fingernails. "I know because I play tennis with the guy in an apartment near hers. I'd met Betts too. Seemed like a nice lady to me."

Nancy leaned toward him. "Did your friend know anything about the murder?"

"Not really," Fitz said. "He thought the sheriff was out of his depth and just fishing. He doesn't have a trained detective on staff."

Louise lifted her chin and sniffed. "I don't think there are any clues except maybe the bullet. What kind of gun, anyone know?"

The faces that looked at her were blank.

Nancy sighed. "We'll have to let the sheriff deal with that and anything that requires technical expertise. We can't analyze a bullet, but he can use the state's facilities to match bullet to gun if he finds the gun. We have to tackle this through knowing the people here and looking for motive and opportunity."

Fitz smiled. "The human touch, you're saying?

Nancy nodded. "Yes, the human touch."

"Who did she pal around with?" Louise pursued.

"Grace Maury, down the hall." Nancy gazed out the window, open for the breezes. The curtains billowed into the dining room. "I'll see if she's available for lunch tomorrow."

Louise flicked her braid. "Yeah. Pick her brains some more."

Nancy bit her lip. Nobody knew anything more about Betts' murder. Disappointing but to be expected. Anyway, they would only be dealing with gossip unless someone had actually seen the sheriff, talked with the sheriff, or picked up a nugget of information directly from the sheriff. And since he couldn't be found around the building and wouldn't divulge anything even if he were, that was unlikely.

Nancy summed it up. "So we'll keep working on the surveys, keep listening to the gossip here, and if any of us sees the sheriff, try to find out what he is doing to solve the murder." She glanced at the others. "Any other ideas?"

"I'll go through the resident directories and see if I spot anyone with a dubious biography," said Louise.

George nodded. "That's a good possibility." He hesitated and frowned. "But now that I think of it, nobody checks those entries for veracity, you know. Left to us to write them and we could say anything. Some people have probably stretched the truth. . .a lot."

'Still, it's a good idea," Nancy said. "Pass the dubious entries on to me and I'll see what I can find out online. Anything else?" Nancy waited. George coughed, Fitz sipped his tea, and Louise stared out the window.

"All right. Since you're all here, I'd like your suggestions on another problem. Nothing to do with the murder, just trying to help out Grace Maury." Nancy brought the clock in from her bedroom. "This is her clock, and it supposedly has a secret. She has no idea what it is and asked for my help. Maybe it's connected to a clue about some Confederate treasure. I've been studying the clock, but haven't found anything to suggest a secret. Any thoughts?"

George whistled. "Confederate treasure, huh?"

Nancy told them Grace's story about the treasure. "I've taken the clock apart and had a watchmaker study it. Neither of us could find any secret. Nothing that looks like a code or cipher; no hidden text; no place to hide anything. What do you think? Any brilliant ideas?"

Fitz pulled the clock toward him and opened the back. He examined the inside, even pulling a magnifying glass out of his tool belt to inspect the works. He shook his head. "Can't imagine what the secret might be," he said. "Nothing out of character here. Did you try a black light on it?"

"Black light?" Nancy gaped at him. "I never thought of that. Just a minute."

She ran into her bedroom, ruffled through several drawers, and returned, holding a small flashlight. "Let's see if something shows up with this."

"What's that?" asked George.

"It's ultraviolet light. I bought this when we were working on that case in Florida." Nancy turned it on and flashed it on the clock. "It shows up some organic stains like urine or blood. . ."

"Ew." George pulled his hands back from the clock. "I'm not touching that. "

"Why would blood or urine be on the clock?" Louise asked.

"Just examples." Nancy took her time to flash the black light all over the clock, inside and out. "I'm thinking a message could be written on it in an organic invisible ink." The search took several minutes, but turned up nothing. Nancy finally turned off the black light. "No luck," she said, hiding her disappointment. She smiled at Fitz. "Good idea, though."

"At least it's clean," George said as he took the clock and studied the dial for several minutes before passing on the clock to Louise, who pushed it back to Nancy. "If you all don't see anything, I sure won't."

Nancy picked up the clock and eyed it at arm's length. Maybe there was no secret at all attached to this clock. A disappointing conclusion but could be the true one. She took it back to her bedroom. An idea might come to her if she put the clock aside for a couple more days. She hated to give up.

***

The next afternoon, Nancy, Louise, and Fitz clustered around George who sat in front of the computer in his den. A two-inch stack of papers was piled to the side. Louise waved a fat manila envelope. "I've got more responses here!"

"Whoo, mon," said Fitz. "We'll be all night."

"Not at all. I set up the database," said George, "with fields that align with the data requested on the survey forms. Okay? Should be a piece of cake."

Nancy picked up several forms. "So now we can input the data. I suggest we each pick up a stack of surveys and take turns giving George the data to put in the fields. By the way, George, what fields did you include?"

George sat back and polished his glasses, squinting at one lens, then the next as he spoke. "Okay. First field is last name, then first name. If it's anonymous, I'll just put an "A" in the spaces." He put his glasses back on and peered at the monitor. "Then apartment number if they give it. Then whether the apartment was occupied by a couple, a man, or a woman. Then type of fraud and in the next field, whether it was by phone, e-mail, mail, or what. I also added a field on whether the fraud succeeded or not and a field for other information." He glanced around at the three watching him. "Anything else?"

Nancy thought a minute. "What about characteristics of the perpetrator? Male, female, accent, country, anything noted about the perp."

"Should have put that on the survey to begin with," Louise said. She pulled the surveys out of the envelope. "I've already leafed through these, and found only five or six different scams mentioned."

George arranged his fingers over the keyboard. "Okay, then. Let's go."

"I'll read through the first batch." Louise looked at Nancy over her glasses. "By the way, fake charitable donation scams seem to be the most common. Then IRS or other government imposter claims.

"All right," said George, drumming his fingers. "Start reading out the data so I can fill in the spreadsheet."

"Keep your pants on." Louise began reading the data off the

sheets, one by one. After twenty-five entries, she passed the stack to Nancy. "Your turn."

Nancy read off the next twenty-five. They took turns until all the data was entered.

As they stretched and sat back, Nancy asked George to do a preliminary sort on type of scams entered.

"Sure," said George. "Might be interesting. He clicked several times, then reached over to pull a sheet from the printer. "Here it is."

Nancy took the sheet and read the results to the group. "Fake charitable donation scams. Ninety-one, including the sheet you've got, Louise."

"Good." Louise said.

"IRS or other government imposter claiming money is owed," Nancy continued. "Twenty-nine."

"Fake grandson or friend in trouble calls and e-mails. Sixty-one. Fake sweepstakes calls. Fifteen."

"And a whole bunch of the Nigerian-type scams. I don't think we should count those," said Louise. "They've been around for decades and really could be from anyplace. We've all gotten them."

"And fake sweepstakes scams." Fitz looked up. "You know, where you get a call saying you've won a lottery or a cruise or some such."

George glanced at Fitz. "How does that work?"

"They tell you that before you can claim the prize you have to pay taxes or some fee first." Nancy said as she straightened the stack of forms. "Once they've got your money, they disappear. You don't get something for nothing."

"No other kinds of scams?" asked Fitz.

"Not in these surveys," Louise said.

"Any comments on the surveys? Additional information that

might be helpful?" Nancy asked. "Everybody pick up a pile of surveys and read through them." She held up a sheet. "This person says she got an e-mail supposedly from E-Z Pass saying she owed for traffic tickets in New Jersey. She said she had been in New Jersey but never got any traffic tickets, so she surfed the Internet and found a website that described this scam."

"She was smart, Luv." Fitz pulled out a form from his pile. "This person said he got a call from someone who said he'd won a sweepstakes prize, and they even sent a check for the first installment, but asked him to pay them for the taxes due. He did, then found out the check they'd sent him was fake. He was too embarrassed to give his name and apartment number."

"I noticed an interesting fact about the fake grandson or friend calls," said Nancy.

They looked at her with interest. "What?" said Louise.

"They were all from a fake grandson, not from a fake granddaughter or a fake friend in trouble. Why do you suppose that was?"

"I'll give you the answer for that. Most of us talk about our grandkids around here. If the perp has a young male relative or friend, what could be easier than to have him impersonate a grandson on the phone? The perp doesn't have a young girl he or she can use. We should look for someone who has a young person visit them frequently."

Nancy shook her head. "They could connect only by e-mail or text, you know." Got to be safer for them if he never shows up here."

Fitz scratched his chin. "That's right. Grandkids, nephews, nieces, all kinds of kids visit Whisperwood. Hard to pinpoint the bad one. Also hard to pull off the fake friend scam by phone. Sending e-mails for emergency help, that is, pleas for money, would work better. A lot of people here travel. Even I've gotten e-mails supposedly from people I know saying they're overseas and been robbed and need money pronto."

"So what did you do?" asked Louise.

Fitz shrugged. "Hit the delete key."

Louise laughed. "Some kind of friend you are."

"Not a friend to crooks, no."

Nancy nodded. "Is it easy to transfer money overseas?"

"Have no idea," Louise said.

"You go to the bank and make a wire transfer," said George. "No big deal."

"I guess even swindlers could have personal preferences. Maybe the scam artist just doesn't like that particular scam." Louise pulled together all the forms.

"The charitable donation scams interest me. Most of the people at Whisperwood hit by this scam didn't fall for it." She paused. "At least that's what they say, but we seniors are a generous bunch. The ones who did respond paid by credit card. On the phone."

Fitz shoved his chair back. "Oh mon. They give them everything with that credit card number."

"All right. George, how about sorting by apartment numbers," Nancy said. "Then we can see if there's a pattern or a cluster of hits around a certain part of the building."

"The anonymous ones didn't include an apartment number." George tapped a few buttons, and another screen appeared. He printed out four copies. "We can all check this out," he said.

They studied the print-outs. "I don't see any pattern or cluster, do you?" said Nancy.

"Nope," said George. 'That's a bust."

Nancy sat back in her chair. "I'm second guessing this one," she said. "You know how most of us are involved in different clubs and activities. Almost all of us know people who live all over the building. If the scammer lives here, he does, too."

Louise nodded. "I think you're right, but if we come up with a suspect, we could see how many organizations that person belongs too. The busier the crooks are, the more people they get to know, and the more targets."

"Good point." Fitz pushed back his chair. "I think we've done about all we can do right now. I've got a doctor's appointment. See you at dinner." He disappeared out the door.

George looked at his watch. "An hour till dinner. So what do we think?" George turned away from the computer screen. "In house or not?"

Nancy pursed her lips in and out as she thought. "Could be in-house. Especially the extortion attempts and the grandson scams, even though there doesn't seem to be a pattern in terms of apartment locations."

"We're not done yet," said Louise.

***

Please Wear Your Name Tags

> Name tags are important at Whisperwood. Be sure to wear yours. The system is designed to be convenient for you and to eliminate the need to carry credit cards on our campus. Name tags help staff bill expenses for dining room guests and special services to the proper party. Name tags also help you remember names of people you've met, thus avoiding embarrassment when you meet again. Thank you.
>
> *-The Whisperwood Breeze, Newsletter for Whisperwood Retirement Village*

CHAPTER 24

Nancy was on her way to the pub for lunch the next day when she bumped into Grace, locking the door of her apartment. "Join me for lunch?" Nancy asked.

Grace smiled at her. "Sure. The pub? I was heading that way. Then I'm off to my investment club meeting. Busy, busy, busy."

"All kinds of things to do here," said Nancy.

They fell into step side by side.

"You said it. Have you made any headway on the clock?" asked Grace.

Nancy shook her head. "I've studied it inside and out and can't find any secret."

"Too bad, but I didn't really see the point anyway." Grace walked into the pub and led the way to a table in back. She wheezed as she settled her heavy bulk into a chair. Nancy took the opposite chair as a server arrived with menus.

"What made you think the clock had a secret?" Nancy took a menu and perused it as she spoke.

Grace was also perusing a menu. "Why does Jefferson want it so much? I know it is valuable, but he is acting like there's more going on with that clock. Can't believe that Confederate treasure story. Anyway, I have the clock, so it's mine. Can't be bothered with

Jefferson's opinion." She stuck out her jaw as if that were the final word on the subject and then peered at Nancy over her glasses.

Finders keepers—the phrase crossed Nancy's mind. "Can you think of anything about that clock's history that might be a clue?"

"Been in the family since before the Civil War." Grace signaled a server. "Our great granddaddy displayed it in the family jewelry store once in a while. That was in Richmond, Virginia, where my family was from." She paused to think. "Maybe it was our great, great granddaddy." She shrugged. "Don't rightly know. But what I heard is that during the Civil War, it helped save the town jewels. Maybe they hid the town treasury and used the clock for that somehow. Must have retrieved the treasury, though. Never heard that it was still missing. There is some secret connected to the clock, but what? That's what drives me nuts."

The server arrived. They gave their orders and Nancy looked back at Grace. "But why do you think so?"

Grace sighed. "The story that came down in my family was that the clock was important for some reason. It might hide the key for what the family did with all the gems and jewelry that were hidden before the rebels burned the town. That's where the story gets a bit confused 'cause it was Hampton, Virginia, that was burned to the ground. And the townspeople torched it." Grace laughed. "They had to do it, you know." She settled back and rearranged the silverware on the table. "Otherwise, the damn Yankees would have stolen everything they could get when they took over Fort Monroe. That was in Hampton and the Yankees held the fort throughout the Civil War. Strategic place for them, being on the coast and all, right at the entrance to the Chesapeake. And the fort was also used as a station on the Underground Railroad."

"Really," Nancy said. What an unusual piece of history. "The Yankees held a fort in the South?"

Grace laughed. "Sure did. Near Norfolk. Hard to believe, isn't it?"

Nancy nodded. "And it was part of the Underground Railroad?" She looked up as the server brought their iced teas.

Grace began spooning sugar into hers. "That's what they say. Of course, you know we're not talking a real railroad, right?"

"I don't know much about it," said Nancy as she sipped the tea.

"Underground Railroad was a metaphor. It was just a chain of safe houses for slaves heading north. The houses were called 'stations.' Fort Monroe was one of them, became one after the general in charge refused to give the runaway slaves hiding there back to the slave owner. This was after Virginia seceded from the Union and war was declared. The general got away with it by calling the slaves "contraband of war." She laughed. "Quite an original and effective gambit, I'd say. So it became a safe house for slaves and hundreds passed through there."

"I don't know too much about the Civil War, except that it was a long time coming and the Union won. Is your family's jewelry store in Richmond still in business?" Nancy asked. "Maybe someone there would know about the clock."

"Sold many, many years ago. Only thing left is that clock, and if it has the key to where the treasure is hidden, I want to know. That's why I refuse to let Jefferson get his hands on it."

Nancy tapped her finger on the table. She could find nothing in the clock that pointed to a hidden stash. "Could the decoration or anything on the clock be a code? Does anything in the design remind you of Hampton?"

"If it did, I would have figured out that clock long time ago." Grace held her glass as the server arrived with their sandwiches.

Nancy hated to give up, but she could not imagine any way that clock could hold a secret she hadn't discovered yet. She bit into her sandwich thoughtfully. "How long had you known Betts?"

"What? Why do you want to know that?" Grace took a long drink of iced tea as she looked at Nancy.

Nancy would have thought the reason was obvious. "Trying to find out more about her. Might lead to who murdered her and why?"

"I have no idea." She chomped into her sandwich. "I don't think it was robbery. Nothing I saw in her apartment was worth stealing. All Ikea stuff. Cheap. What wasn't from Pier 1 Imports. All that African stuff. And I never saw her wearing expensive jewelry." She looked up at Nancy. "I do miss her though," she said as she eyed the second half of her sandwich.

"Did you know any of her friends?" Nancy considered Grace's offhand attitude as she studied Grace's body language. Nancy had once thought Grace and Betts were close friends, but Grace's comments told a different story. Was Grace just trying to distance herself from a murder victim? Some people did that. And Nancy hadn't seen any Ikea furniture in the apartment. Of course, Betts' family might have taken out her furniture, while the African furnishings belonged to Samira.

"I didn't hang around with her much," said Grace, dabbing at her mouth with a napkin. "Didn't associate with her friends. Not really my kind, you know?" She smiled at Nancy.

Nancy's mind buzzed with various interpretations of this statement, but she'd realized a long time ago that judgmental statements shut people up. It was more important to find out exactly what Grace did think.

"Oh?" Nancy said. "I thought you two were really good friends."

"Not really, but I was curious about her." Grace picked up the dessert card and looked around for the server. "She seemed sneaky to me, devious. Like she was really a cop or something."

Nancy sat back in surprise. If Grace thought that about her, why had she acted like such a chum? When Nancy had first met them, she had felt an undercurrent of something withheld and unstated. Perhaps there was a mutual feeling of dislike. What had Betts thought about Grace? Nancy would never know, but many African-Americans had a healthy distrust of white people and their motives. Rightly so, it seemed.

***

Wednesday Night
Happy Hour &
Tropical Night at the Pub
Featured drink this Wednesday:
Mango Rum Splash
4 to 6 p.m.
Join your friends for
Happy Hour before dinner.
Wine and beer: Two for the price of one!
Appetizers too!

- *Billboard Notice at the Pub*

CHAPTER 25

Nancy left Grace in the lobby after lunch and took the elevator to the third floor. On the hall shelf outside Jefferson's apartment, a miniature Confederate flag hung defiantly and against Whisperwood guidelines from a foot-high flagpole. Circling the base was a stem of silk dogwood blossoms. Nancy dredged up a memory that the dogwood was Virginia's state flower.

Helen answered the door and invited her into one of the more spacious apartments at Whisperwood, but the feeling of space was stillborn in the living room's expensive but oppressive decoration. Drab early American furniture crowded the room, and heavy three-tiered draperies obscured most of the window space, leaving glints of sunlight like theatre spotlights in the gloom.

They were drinking martinis. It was too early for that for Nancy, but Jefferson poured her one before she could refuse, so she accepted it as she sat on the couch. Helen took a seat in an armchair, peering at Nancy over her glass but saying nothing. She looked like a spider ready to pounce on a fly.

Jefferson remained standing by the liquor cabinet. He lifted his glass to her. "To what do we owe this visit, Nancy?"

"I just had lunch with Grace," Nancy began.

"What's she done now?" asked Helen, putting a cigarette in her mouth and letting it dangle unlit.

Their apartment didn't reek of cigarette smoke, and Nancy noticed a clean ashtray on the coffee table. Those used to be popular items, scattered around everyone's house. Nancy hadn't seen one in years. Maybe Jefferson and Helen didn't smoke indoors. Then Nancy remembered that Jefferson had worked for the tobacco industry, but she had never seen him smoking. Maybe they both pretended to smoke as protective coloring while Jefferson worked for a tobacco company. Shabby ethics if that were the case.

Good thing Louise hadn't come with her, Nancy thought. She would have alienated Jefferson and Helen in two seconds. Discussing Betts with these two would be dicey enough. "We talked about Grace's friend Betts," Nancy said. "I'd only met her once and liked her. I wish I'd known her better." She soft-peddled, hoping to draw them out. "Did you know her at all?"

Jefferson snorted. "Betts wasn't Grace's friend unless Grace wanted something from her."

Nancy tucked this judgment away to explore later. Is that the way Grace really was or only Jefferson's jaundiced opinion? She bypassed the comment. "Do you know of any reason why someone would kill Betts?"

Helen put down her unlit cigarette and laughed. "So is Little Miss Detective on the job again?" Her voice reeked of alcohol-spawned belligerency.

Nancy sat up and crossed her legs. "I'm sure the sheriff has the investigation well in hand. I'm just filling in some of the background for him." Helen must be on her second drink. What would she say next? "I thought you might have known Betts better than me and might have some ideas."

"I don't consort with people like her," said Jefferson.

"Absolutely not," added Helen.

"She seemed like a pleasant person to me," said Nancy. "Quite sharp. Witty."

"I'm not a bigot, if that's what you're implying," said Jefferson. "But I do have my principles and I don't like people who snoop. I stayed away from her." He raised an eyebrow at Nancy. "And I'm keeping an eye on you."

Helen tittered. "We have nothing to hide, but we don't put up with unsocial, nasty behavior from anyone. That applies regardless of race, color, religion, political affiliation, or," she paused for the finish, "sexual orientation." She tittered again. "Just like the government."

"That's enough, Helen." Jefferson frowned at her.

"Someone murdered her," Nancy said. "You say she snooped?"

"Yes, I say she snooped." Jefferson folded his arms. "She must have found out something that disagreed with her health." He laughed.

"But not us," Helen added. She waved her hand loosely, as drunks do. "What you see is what we got."

Jefferson left the liquor cabinet and sat in the other armchair. "If I were you, I'd be a darn sight more careful about who I talked to."

Nancy took a small sip of her martini, hiding her distaste for the drink. Anyway, she couldn't drink more than a few sips if she wanted to do all her errands that afternoon. She changed the subject. "Why is the old clock so important to you?"

Jefferson sat back, glass in one hand and flicking at a piece of lint on his slacks with the other. "Of course I want that clock. It's part of our family history. Did you know they used to put it in the family jewelry store window in Richmond now and then?" He crossed his legs and leaned toward Nancy, emphasizing his words with his index finger. "They did that from the first time they bought the thing and that was before the War of Northern Aggression. Kept it in the window until we sold the store. Took the clock home with us."

He leaned back against the chair and stretched his arm out along the back. "People would stop by just to stare at that clock. Hardly anyone could afford a watch in those days. We all knew how expensive it was and that it came from France. Our great granddaddy," he hesitated, "or maybe it was our great great granddaddy," he shook his head, "doesn't matter, bought it when he was over there for our government." He stopped and took a deep breath. "History. That's what it's all about."

Nancy gazed around the room at the collection of historical artifacts on the credenza, the highboy and the bookshelves. Maybe history was what it was all about for Jefferson. "Are there any other stories about the clock? Like maybe it has a code in it? Or some other kind of secret message?"

Jefferson snorted. "Grace been talking to you? Ridiculous. She probably told you that old yarn about Confederate treasure. There's a bunch of hooey for you. There's no secret in that clock. It's just a handsome, well-made mantel clock. That's all it is."

"Really." Helen laughed. "And as soon as we get it back, we'll move out of this dump!"

***

Sign Up Now for Summer Trips

The World Wanderers, Whisperwood's travel club, is accepting applications for its summer list of one, two, three and seven day excursions.

Reserve your place now. The trips fill up fast.

You don't want to miss out!

Here's where the club is going this summer. The full itinerary and cost of all excursions are posted on the lobby bulletin board. A flyer and application may be picked up at the reception desk.

- Bus tour of tidewater Virginia, including a boat trip to the historic island of Tangier in the Chesapeake, and a day at historic Williamsburg. Seven days. Includes breakfast and two dinners. Other meals on your own.
- Bus trip to historic Williamsburg. Two days. Breakfast included.
- Bus trip to tour Charlestown, WV's capital. Includes stop at a coal mine. One day.
- Bus trip to Washington, D.C., to visit the Smithsonian museums on the mall. Three days. Includes theater tickets to a performance at Arena Stage and all breakfasts.
- Bus trip and tour of Annapolis and Baltimore. Includes luncheon at the Annapolis harbor, visit to Baltimore's Visionary Art Museum, and all breakfasts. Seven days.

- The Whisperwood Breeze, Newsletter for Whisperwood retirement Village

CHAPTER 26

Nancy left the Tophams and mulled over her impressions. They were courteous on the surface, but she could feel the undercurrents. They'd brought up the buried Confederate treasure, probably because they figured Grace had mentioned it, then scoffed at it. Of course they would. No sense giving anyone the idea that there might be truth to the story.

Nancy passed through the lobby, waving to Louise and George working together at the table to collect signatures and scam stories. She smiled, thinking how their relationship had grown. She felt happy for them both even though the memories of Bill and her own loss shadowed her thoughts at the same time.

She continued down the hall. Grace's door opened and two men stepped out, followed by Grace. She saw Nancy and stopped, glancing at the two men. Richard Maury. Grace's husband. Who was the younger man?

"Nancy! I didn't expect. . ." Grace looked at Richard as if for reassurance. He bowed slightly, a faint smile crossing his face.

"Miss Nancy. Nice to see you again. I didn't know you were a famous detective." He put one arm around Grace and extended his hand. Nancy shook it. Richard seemed fit and tanned. He was taller than Grace, and he wore a yellow polo shirt with sharply creased navy blue slacks and black loafers. He looked as if he were on his way to the golf course. "Been hearing so much about you from Grace."

Nancy laughed. "Not famous. Long retired. I'm pleased to see you again, Richard."

"And this is my nephew, Alex."

Alex came forward and nodded with a slight smile. He seemed about twenty years old and wore a white T-shirt with pressed jeans and black and white running shoes. His thumbs were hooked onto the belt loops, giving him a slight swagger.

Nancy smiled at him, but he glanced away without speaking. The swagger was just show, Nancy decided. He was probably shy. She turned back to Richard, who seemed to be as smooth as a car salesman. A car salesman wouldn't earn enough to afford this place, but a high-powered executive would probably be a smooth, slick, and courteous talker. She waited curiously to see how Richard responded.

Grace spoke first. "They were just leaving."

Nancy saw a silent message pass between her and Richard. Alex started down the hall.

Richard nodded. "Yes, we were." He glanced at his watch. "Got a golf date at the clubhouse. Nice to have met you, Ms. Dickenson." He followed Alex down the hall, turning back once to wave at Grace. "See you later."

She ignored the wave. "How about coming in for a few minutes, Nancy?"

Nancy's curiosity bump itched. Something was going on here. She hardly ever saw Richard around. Maybe they were separated and kept up a facade. She knew a few couples who did that. "Just for a few minutes." Nancy followed Grace into the apartment.

"Alex came over to help us move out of here," Grace said, sinking into the wicker armchair. Nancy sat on the red-flowered couch.

"You're moving out?" Nancy saw a stack of boxes against a wall. "Why? Harry's added more security guards to patrol the grounds and halls. The killer will be found soon. We're all perfectly safe here."

Grace clasped and unclasped her hands, then she began twisting the ring around on her finger. "Are we?" she asked in a small voice. "I'm afraid and I want to get out of here."

Nancy nodded. "We're all upset at what happened to Betts."

"It could have been any of us!" Grace said.

Nancy shook her head. "I don't think so. Betts found out something that was dangerous to someone. That's why she was killed."

Grace stared at Nancy with open mouth. "Why do you say that? It could be a serial killer and Betts was his first victim here. That's what I think." She reached for the tissues on the coffee table and blew her nose. "And that's what other people think, too!"

"What other people?" asked Nancy. Whoever the killer was, it would be to his or her advantage to throw suspicion onto someone who killed out of an insane compulsion. She leaned forward. "Tell me. Who are these people who think it's a serial killer?"

Grace drew back as if to keep Nancy away. "People. People I talk to in the dining room and the halls. Everyone's talking about it."

"I see." She needed to pass this on to Harry immediately. Whisperwood couldn't afford a mass exodus. He had hired extra security guards, installed more lighting on the grounds, and instructed staff to alert the security chief if they saw anyone acting suspiciously. But he hadn't communicated these measures to the residents. He was still too green to realize how necessary that was. The residents needed to feel secure and safe.

"Anyway, you might not want to leave yet," Nancy added. "The sheriff will wonder if you had something to do with it." A far-fetched notion, but if it helped Grace get through this rough patch, she'd probably thank Nancy for pushing her into staying.

Whisperwood was a nice place to live. Most of the time. Of course, someone did set a fire in the auditorium, and none of the security guards had seen that happen. Nancy was convinced that the sole purpose of the fire was to discourage the dissemination of information about consumer fraud. Once they caught the scam operator here, they would also have the arsonist and Betts' murderer. The three crimes had to be connected. As soon as the perpetrator was behind bars, Whisperwood would again become a safe protected environment. Harry had warned Nancy to keep quiet about the arson. The official word had been that the fire was caused by a faulty wire and had been repaired.

Grace's face had turned white. She clutched a trembling hand to her heart. "Wh-a-a-t did you say?" she stammered. "Me? Never. I was her friend." She took a deep breath and gripped the arms of the chair with both hands. "I was one of her few friends, Nancy." She took another deep breath. "Maybe you're right. Betts could be nosy and obnoxious. Maybe she did find out someone's secret. But me? I don't have any secrets."

Nancy smiled. Everyone had secrets.

Grace closed her eyes and leaned back in the chair as if to steady herself. Her lips moved as if she were counting to herself, or maybe saying a prayer, then she opened her eyes. "In fact, you must be right. It's the only thing that makes sense. Betts learned someone's secret, something that would send that person to jail—she was such a law and order person, you know?" Grace looked at Nancy as if for confirmation. "A snitch. She would have gone to the sheriff or the FBI or whoever, that's what she would have done—and that's why she was murdered. Nobody likes a snitch."

"I think you're right." Nancy nodded. "And that's why you're safe." Nancy crossed her fingers. "You don't know that kind of secret."

Grace looked down at her hands, "That's right. I don't know any kind of secret." She hesitated and smiled at Nancy. "That would hurt anyone, I mean."

"I'm sure the sheriff is closing in on the criminal. He must be responsible for the fire, too. Every crime that person commits will increase the clues that will trap him."

Grace smiled. "I'm sure you're right. I'll talk to Richard. Maybe we could hold off moving." She stuck out her jaw. "After all, we don't know anything."

Nancy left the apartment hoping that Grace would now help stop the gossip mill from starting a stampede out of Whisperwood, but they needed to ferret out the murderer soon.

***

Whisperwood's New Hotline: 555-0001

> No matter how wrong a rumor may be, it can spread as fast as spilled water and seep into every crevice of human conversation. Whisperwood has established a hot line, staffed by the counseling center, to provide correct information on any aspect of life at Whisperwood that is troubling you. You also can help by not passing on gossip and rumors. Check with the Hotline and get it right!
>
> \- *The Whisperwood Breeze, Newsletter for Whisperwood Retirement Village*

Chapter 27

As Nancy approached her own apartment, she could hear Malone's pathetic cries and hoped the neighbors didn't. What was eating him now? He acted like that when something was wrong. Could someone have broken in? She checked her door lock and noted scratches on it, but her door was still locked and secure as always. A thief might not have expected to encounter the heavy-duty lock on Nancy's door since most door locks at Whisperwood were simple and easily opened by someone who knew what he was doing. Residents felt secure enough with their friendly neighbors and patrolling security guards, but after several close calls the year before, Nancy, Louise, and George had installed deadbolts instead.

She opened the door with her key as usual. Nothing was amiss, although. . . . she took another look at the additional stack of forms on her dining room table. They were still coming in. She just hadn't taken these over to George yet. She remembered the one she'd left on top. She shuffled through the pile to find it somewhere in the middle.

Malone's cries had turned to whining meows from behind the bedroom door. She hadn't closed him in the bedroom when she left. She rarely did that anymore unless he hovered near the hall door in a bid to escape. She checked the windows and found the answer. The screen on the living room window had been sliced across the bottom and side. Nancy remembered leaving the windows open for the warm spring breezes. Easy to climb through the ground floor window, then whoever it was somehow enticed Malone into the bedroom. He was a sucker for any kind of treat.

Malone cried piteously again. Could Malone have been hurt? Nancy rushed to open the bedroom door. Malone lay curled on the floor by a pool of vomit. Drool hung from his jaw. He moaned as he looked up at her with pitiful eyes. He acted as if he needed her, wanted her to help him. He had never done that before. Malone was such an independent cat, he must really be sick. Nancy reached down to comfort Malone. In the vomit she could see bits of what might be meat or fish and green flecks. Green flecks? Had the meat been poisoned?

Malone moaned and tried to stand, but he fell over as he heaved. She ran into the kitchen, grabbed a couple of plastic bowls, and used a spoon to scrape some of the vomit and the meat with the green flecks into the bowls, which she covered and placed in a bag. She picked up Malone, wrapped him in a towel, and cuddled him, something he never allowed, as she raced with him and the bag down the hall to Fitz's apartment. She banged on the door, praying he was home.

"Just a moment," a voice called out from within. A few seconds later, the door opened. Fitz took one look at Nancy's distraught face and the bundle in her arms and reached for her. "Something wrong with Malone?"

"He's been poisoned," Nancy said, holding Malone closer.

"Let's go." Fitz led Nancy and Malone out to the parking lot to his sky-blue Cadillac. He helped Nancy settle onto the seat with Malone in her arms before running around to the driver's side.

"Where's the vet?" he asked as he buckled his seat belt.

Nancy felt tears pricking at her eyelids. She had never seen Malone looking so sick and so pitiful. Thank goodness Fitz had come through. "Just this side of town. Sorry to drag you out, but I'm afraid to drive my own car right now."

She stroked Malone's back. He had stopped throwing up, but he felt limp in her arms. She glanced at the soft blue upholstery of the seat. Fitz knew what was important.

"Don't blame you. We have to catch the culprits before we can go back to life as usual." Fitz whipped out through the gate and sped down the mountain road. "No telling how they might have booby-trapped your car since the mechanics returned it."

"You're not as prominent as Louise and I," Nancy said. "They won't expect you to drive me. Your car must be safe from them."

Fitz chuckled. "Incognito. That's what I am."

"They broke into my apartment, and they poisoned Malone." The poor cat wasn't moving. Nancy held him closer, terrified that he wouldn't make it. She glanced at Fitz and then at the speedometer. He was going as fast as possible on this curving mountain road.

The drive took twenty minutes. Nancy pointed out the vet's clinic and Fitz drove up to the door. He sprang out of the car and ran around to Nancy's side to help her with Malone.

"Emergency," Nancy called out as she rushed into the vet's office. "My cat's been poisoned."

"Poisoned? Oh, the poor thing," said the receptionist, as she saw the pitiful bundle in Nancy's arms. "Take him into Room A," she told Nancy, then she ran into the back yelling, "Dr. Amos."

Dr. Amos nodded at Nancy as he walked in to examine Malone. "You say he vomited several times?"

Nancy nodded as she stroked Malone to comfort him. He had to be all right. Nancy couldn't fathom life without him. He connected her to Bill, but he was a personality himself. He had to be okay.

"Did you bring some of the vomit?" He peered at Nancy over his bifocals. "And whatever he ate that was bad?"

Nancy gave him the bag. She watched him open the containers, sniff at the contents, then study the meat." He looked at Nancy. "Just as I thought. Rat poison."

"Rat poison!"

"See those little green bits?" He pointed them out with a pencil. "They crushed the pellets and mixed them with the food." He raised an eyebrow at Nancy. "Has Malone been a bad kitty? Bothered the neighbors?"

Nancy shook her head. "I don't let him out of the apartment."

Dr. Amos laid a hand on Malone and looked at Nancy. "He got into something nasty, but he seems to have thrown it all up."

Yeah. Nancy had first-hand experience with that. Any cat food mix he didn't like, for instance. For once Nancy felt grateful for Malone's propensity to throw up.

"He'll be all right, but I'll give him a vitamin K shot." He nodded at his assistant.

She looked at him and left the room.

Dr. Amos turned to Nancy. "Let me keep him overnight for observation. He'll sleep it off." He handed her a vial of pills. "Vitamin K. Give him one of these a day for a month.

Nancy leaned down and hugged Malone, stroking his back. "Thank you, doctor." She turned away, feeling too shaken to say anything more. "I'm just going to sit in your waiting room for a few minutes if you don't mind."

"Of course," said Dr. Amos. "Malone is too tough a cat to let a little case of poisoning get to him. He'll be fine tomorrow."

Nancy nodded. She sat in one of the waiting room chairs next to Fitz, who held her hand in comfort.

She returned to an apartment that seemed quiet and deserted as if all the life had gone out of it. Malone filled up the environment. For all his faults, he was a companion and, as Nancy had realized before to her surprise, she loved him.

Nancy searched her bedroom as soon as she returned from the vet and found another tiny remnant of fish on the floor. She cleaned up the mess and then searched the apartment for signs of theft, but nothing appeared to have been taken. The burglars had looked through the bureau drawers in her bedroom, rummaged through the cubby holes in her desk, and shuffled through the pile of survey forms. They were prepared to get Malone out of the way with the poisoned meat they'd brought with them, so the break-in was not a random event by outsiders.

Thinking of poor Malone made her feel like crying. She reminded herself that he would be okay and she'd have him back the next day. The thought made her smile at the irony. Who would have thought that she'd learn to love such an arrogant, demanding pain of a cat?

She walked back to the living room, leaned against the wall, and folded her arms. What were they searching for? Did they find it? Nothing appeared to be missing, but they had looked through the forms and didn't take them. Why not? Were they just interested in what the residents had written? Apparently so, but poisoning Malone made the crime more than one of idle curiosity.

She stepped into the kitchen. She didn't like to waste food, but Fitz was right. Anything could be added to an open sugar bowl, salt shaker, bottle of milk, whatever. She threw out the sugar, salt, pepper, and the contents of bottles and jars that were open.

Then to divert her thoughts from worrying about Malone, Nancy walked into the bedroom to again examine the clock. The thief could have taken it but did not, so the clock was not the object of the thief's break-in. Still, it was obviously valuable, so why wouldn't they take it? She sat at the dressing table and ran through the now familiar inventory of clock possibilities. Did it hold the key to Confederate treasure? Were the porcelain flowers some kind of code? If so, she'd need the appropriate code book, which she did not have, to find any answers. Nothing in any pattern indicated Morse code. The hands were elaborately filigreed, but they were easy to remove and replaced with perhaps hands of a simpler design. That could be a code but, again, no code book. The maker's name had been stamped inside the case, but there were no other markings on the works and all the mechanical parts seemed to have a function. Nothing extra that could have significance. Again she gave up and returned the clock to her dressing room table.

Another thought occurred to her. Could diamonds or some other valuable have been added to the clay when the porcelain clock case and flower decorations were made? They would have to withstand the firing in the kiln. If that were so, the case and flowers would have to be destroyed to retrieve the gems. Nancy discarded the idea. Too far-fetched and to find out if that were the clock's secret, they would have to demolish a valuable antique. Not going to happen.

Considerably calmer, she called George. His gruff voice barked, "Hay-lo. If this is a solicitation, I will hang up."

"Check your caller ID, George," Nancy said. "I need to bring the rest of the forms over to you."

"Sure. I'll be here," said George. "You sound upset. Is everything okay?"

Nancy told him about Malone. "I think they were after the forms, so I need to get them out of here right now. No one knows you've got them."

"You're right." George paused before adding, "We need to keep it that way."

***

Nancy met Louise outside the dining room as they waited for the hostess to seat them.

"Any word on the trip we signed up for?" Louise asked.

"I forgot to tell you," said Nancy. "I got a letter from them today."

"Ah ha!" said Louise, a wicked gleam in her eyes. "What did they say?"

"They are taking the high road." Nancy grinned at Louise. "It was a long letter, explaining the rigors of the trip, the need for tough hiking shoes, the lack of accommodations for walkers, wheelchairs, and disabilities, the stairs we'll be climbing, etc." She laughed. "You might think they were trying to talk us out of the trip."

"I don't doubt that, but they are accepting us?" asked Louise.

Nancy extended her hand. "Looks like we're on for a trip to Maine and Nova Scotia." They shook hands.

"All right!" Louise gave the time-honored thumbs-up. "We'll show 'em."

Fitz arrived, then George, a symphony in pink. Nancy smiled at his outfit. Pink bow tie, pink shirt, pink slacks. She glanced at Louise who put up her hands as if to say, "It's not my fault."

They followed their student hostess Taneesha to their usual table, number fifty-six. As they took their seats, Nancy couldn't help smiling at George's outfit. He brightened their table and her heart. She had donned navy blue slacks and a powder blue blouse that enhanced her white curly hair and pale complexion. Louise wore gray slacks, black T-shirt, and her trademark khaki vest. She had pinned a button on the vest that said, "Grow Organic." Her long gray braid hung down her back as usual.

Taneesha hovered at their table a little too long. She seemed to want to say something. Nancy smiled at her. "How's it going?"

"Everything's fine," said Taneesha. She cleared her throat nervously. "I'd like to ask you, uh, that is . . ."

"Go ahead, shoot," said Louise, unfolding the napkin in her lap.

"I, uh, graduate the end of May, you know. . ." began Taneesha, her hands tight on the stack of menus she held.

"Got all your papers in for college?" asked Nancy. Taneesha was too bright not to continue her education, and Whisperwood helped with scholarships.

Taneesha nodded. "What I'd like," she began, "that is, can you all come to my graduation?"

"Wow," said Louise. "I'd love to."

Nancy nodded and George and Fitz chimed in. "Me too."

Nancy got up and hugged her. "We're thrilled for you," she said.

Taneesha gave a sign of relief. "Thank you. You don't know how much that means to me."

"We think you're wonderful," said Nancy, who had tapped Taneesha's powers of observation, curiosity, and intelligence in the past. "You're going to go far."

Taneesha glanced at the reception desk. "Oops. Gotta get back. I'll give you the details later when I know them."

She raced away as George signaled the dining room manager to order wine. The manager arrived and took their orders as the student server came for their food orders. The special that evening was tilapia with shrimp sauce, one of Nancy's favorites. George and Fitz ordered the baked chicken, and Louise ordered the vegetarian lasagna. "Something for everyone," she commented as she usually did.

"Someone broke into my apartment today," Nancy announced after the server left. "And poisoned Malone."

"Poisoned Malone!" Louise stared at Nancy in dismay. "Is he okay?"

Nancy took a sip of water. "He's at the vet's for observation. I pick him up tomorrow. The vet says he'll be fine."

"How did that happen?" asked George. "I like that feisty little guy."

"Whoever broke in threw a piece of poisoned meat into the bedroom."

Louise groaned. "Malone couldn't resist and the burglar locked him in. Right?

Nancy nodded. "I don't know what the burglar was looking for, but I don't think he took anything. He did read through the survey forms, though."

"I didn't hear anything unusual in the hall today," said Fitz. "Course, I usually don't."

"They broke in through the window from outside. Our door locks are too strong."

"Makes me glad I live on the fourth floor," said Louise.

George pursed his lips. "Since he didn't take anything, then he must have wanted to look at those forms. Just wanted to see what kind of information we're bringing in. "

"That's what I think," said Nancy. "Anyway, you now have all of them, and we're the only ones who know that."

George sat back and patted his stomach. "I've been going over the data, and I'm pretty sure the data show that whoever is behind these scams lives here at Whisperwood." George grinned at them, then turned as the manager brought their wine. He raised his glass in a toast. "To the 90s Club."

The glasses clinked as Fitz turned to Nancy. "So did you throw out everything that could have been tampered with? They could have put poison in your sugar or milk. . ."

Nancy nodded. "Thank you for mentioning that." She took a sip and set her glass down.

"As you know," she said with a smile, "I like to read mysteries."

Louise drew back in mock surprise. "No! You?"

"I am shocked," said George.

"All right." Nancy sipped her wine. "I read all sorts of mysteries, but I do enjoy Aaron Elkins' books, where he talks about 'interconnected monkey business.' If you have one bit of funny business here and another bit there, the law of the universe says they're connected."

"I get it," said Fitz. "We've got a bunch of scams that seem to originate with someone here and. . ."

"And we've got a murder," broke in Louise.

"And we have three attempts on my life," added Nancy.

"Don't forget the fire in the auditorium," put in Fitz. "That was arson. The only reason to destroy the auditorium was to prevent the presentation by the woman from the State Attorney's Office."

George nodded. "It's too much of a coincidence if they are not related."

"Yes," said Nancy, "interconnected monkey business. Betts may have found out who the scammer was and got killed for it."

"You have a reputation here." Louise flipped her braid. "Especially after last year. Top-notch detective, that's what they think of you. Any crooks planning scams and committing murders here would want to get rid of you."

George nodded. "Makes sense to me."

"Me too," said Fitz.

"Betts must have known that person or persons pretty well," said Fitz.

Louise shook her head. "Not necessarily—she could have found out by accident just wandering the halls."

Nancy frowned as she studied her wineglass. "Whoever it is, how would they operate? They'd have to work in their apartment, probably with those anonymous cell phones anyone can buy." She looked at George. "How many scam calls were from a woman and how many from a man?"

"Don't forget a young man or teenager," said Louise. "The grandson in Mexico scam that hit Marie, for instance. She said the voice sounded young, like her grandson. An old person like one of us couldn't fake that."

George pursed his lips. "We didn't exactly ask that question."

"It has to be a network, doesn't it? Several people involved," said Fitz.

"A couple? Man and wife?" suggested George.

Nancy looked at George. "What about location of the victims. Did they seem to center on a certain area of the building?"

George shook his head. "Nope, but then the way we all wander around this building helps all of us connect with each other. Designed that way, you know. Pool, gym, garden, dining room, pub, billiard room, library—are scattered around the building, and we all visit those places. Lot of intermingling."

"One of the things I like about this place," put in Fitz.

"Me, too," said Nancy, tapping her fingers on the tablecloth, "but I think we should do more to identify the people and groups Betts hung around with and start checking into them."

Louise turned to her. "You need to watch your step, stay around other people, keep your eyes open. You are a threat to someone here, and whoever that is, after three failed attempts, he'll make sure he succeeds the next time."

***

Activities Fair Next Wednesday

Looking for something to do? Whisperwood has clubs, groups, and activities to meet any interest. Sports, music, games, community welfare—all these and more are available right here. The Activities Fair will be held on Wednesday from 10 a.m. until 12 noon in the lobby. Activity sponsors and members will be available to tell you about their activity at tables set up with flyers, brochures, and sign-up sheets.

Activities Fair
Wednesday, 10 till 12, Lobby

- *The Whisperwood Breeze, Newsletter for Whisperwood Retirement Village*

CHAPTER 28

The next morning Nancy brought Malone home from the vet and made sure he was settled with an old blanket and a bowl of his favorite cat food. She left him sleeping and walked to the window, noting the repair made by Whisperwood's maintenance staff. The Security Patrol had promised to keep an even more watchful eye on her apartment.

Nancy called Samira. She might know about Betts' friends and acquaintances or at least some of them.

"I don't know how you got that idea, Nancy," Samira said. "We were colleagues at work and hung around together a lot, but after we moved here, we more or less went our separate ways." She paused before adding with a slight laugh, "Better that way, if you get me."

Nancy frowned. Was Samira trying to back away from any involvement with Betts? Afraid that association might bring the murderer to her? Nancy had met other people, superstitious people, who tried to ward off trouble that way.

"She was a cop at heart, Nancy," Samira added. "I left all that behind me when I retired. Saw too much of it then. Not interested."

Nancy stared at the phone. "But you would have wanted to stop any crime being committed here, wouldn't you?"

"But was there crime being committed here?" Samira asked. "Or was Betts just seeing something that wasn't there, interfered in something that was none of her business? Somebody's secret that had nothing to do with anything happening here. And then she paid for it."

Unconnected monkey business? Nancy didn't believe it for a minute. Odd that Samira would put forth that point of view. Samira sounded more like a timid suburban housewife than the seasoned law officer she was supposed to be. Is that what a cushy protected lifestyle did to people? It was hard to keep the censure out of her tone, "Betts was a decent person, a nice person, and I liked her. The more I learn about her, the more I respect her. I want her killer found."

Samira's tone turned cold. "Don't judge me like that. I liked and respected her, too. She still was obnoxious and nosy. I could have killed her myself a few times. Not that I did," she added.

Get a grip, Nancy told herself. "I'm just trying to find out who her friends are so I can talk to them. They might know something."

Samira's voice became frigid. "You'll have to ask someone else. We didn't pal around together here." Then she hung up.

Nancy called Ruth Smith with the same question. "Sorry, Nancy," Ruth said, "she was a pleasant neighbor and I liked her, but I didn't really know her or her friends." She paused, then added, "You know how it is here. We meet friends for dinner or games in the common areas but rarely have a party in our own apartments."

Nancy nodded. She had wondered why that was so.

"That's the way you might find out about her special friends," said Ruth. "Otherwise, if you were observant, you might notice who she palled around with, but I wasn't. Why would I? I don't even know who she went to dinner with most of the time."

Then Nancy called Grace, but Grace didn't answer. Nancy couldn't think of anyone else who might have known Betts well. She debated with herself and finally called Samira back, ready to eat humble pie. Samira didn't answer. Nancy left a message of apology and then asked Samira to join her for lunch at the pub. Nancy hung up the phone. Would Samira meet her in the pub? Or snub her and ignore the invitation?

Nancy walked over to her computer. She was stymied in finding Betts' friends, but she could do a background check on Betts, Jefferson, and others in that circle. She checked the criminal databases first, but she suspected that anyone with a criminal record would have changed his or her name. They probably could not afford to live here anyway. She did find a DUI conviction for Jefferson's wife Helen, but that was almost five years ago.

Other searches turned up several articles written by Jefferson on topics relating to the history of Richmond, Virginia. Nothing on Grace or Ruth. Betts received a commendation for her work with the Department of Justice, and several articles on legal issues mentioned her name. Nothing on Samira.

If Jefferson was convinced that the clock held the secret to hidden Confederate treasure, then he might be driven to steal the clock or perhaps harass Grace until she gave it to him. But why would he kill Betts? Whoever broke into Nancy's apartment could easily have stolen the clock if that was his aim, but he didn't. He was more interested in the survey forms detailing the residents' experiences with consumer fraud. Would Jefferson be mixed up in consumer fraud? He was a racist. Would he have murdered Betts in a frenzy of racial hatred? He didn't seem the type.

And what about Samira? She was Betts' roommate. Relations between roommates can get pretty intense but murderous? Betts could conceivably have found out about a secret, maybe even a criminal secret, that Samira was trying to hide. Samira herself was the one who brought up that possibility, and it could be a motive for murder.

Could Grace have a motive to kill Betts? Grace claimed not to know Betts well, but that was not the impression Nancy received when Grace and Betts showed up together at her door.

Why deny it then? Grace seemed afraid of being murdered herself. Did she know why Betts had been murdered? Did that make Grace a target too? Is that what she was afraid of?

What about opportunity? Betts was found shot in the shrubbery behind the building. The place was accessible to everyone, and she'd been killed sometime during the night or early morning. If so, it had to be before the early joggers were out. Easy to wait until the coast was clear, since the joggers all tended to run together and most of the jogging path ran along the perimeter of the property and through the woods. The joggers could alibi each other, but none of Nancy's suspects belonged to that intrepid group. The sheriff must have interviewed them without result and probably had the autopsy results and an accurate time of death by now. He hadn't shared it with her or Harry—Harry would have told her. Since she'd helped him save his skin through the fiasco last year, he'd been a loyal ally and friend.

Could she visit the sheriff and ask questions? Would he answer them?

Lack of an alibi was not going to help pinpoint the murderer. Everyone could claim to be asleep at the time. And Betts could have been held prisoner until a convenient time to kill her.

The weapon had not been found, but Betts had probably been shot with a small handgun, such as anyone might carry for self-defense. It must have had a silencer, since no one heard the shot. Again, the sheriff hadn't divulged any details.

The phone rang. Samira. She agreed to meet Nancy at the pub in an hour for lunch. Nancy checked her watch and petted Malone. He seemed more subdued than usual and even allowed Nancy to snuggle with him for a few minutes before she left to explore the murder site on her way to lunch.

The site was easy to find, identified by the yellow tape surrounding a patch of shrubs and trees behind the building. No one guarded the site, and by this time, the tape was frayed and torn. Nancy felt no compunction at stepping across it and looking around for herself. Obviously the sheriff and his deputies had fine-combed the area, and if they found anything, were not going to divulge it to her. C'est la vie.

A dark patch on the ground marked the spot where Betts must have lain. Nancy thought of Betts' vibrant spirit, her intelligence, forever stilled. A wave of sadness crossed her soul until anger took over. How dare someone take Betts' life. The arrogance of it made Nancy clench her fists. Whoever it was, they were not going to get away with it. She studied the ground as she walked in widening circles in the probably useless search for any clue left behind. The sheriff's deputies had been thorough. Nancy found nothing that might lead to the murderer.

She stopped once again at the dark spot on the grass and surveyed the scene around her, shading her eyes against the sun. Why was this spot chosen?

She answered her own question. Surrounded by shrubs and trees, it could not be seen from the building, and it was accessible from any of the ground floor apartments with terraces or from the back doors of the building.

Nancy strolled back to the building, deep in thought. What had Betts found out the day or night before her death?

When Nancy arrived at the pub, Samira was already sipping a

glass of wine. Nancy ordered chardonnay. They both spent a moment perusing the menu and quickly gave their orders when the server arrived.

Nancy was anxious to appease. Apparently Samira was also.

"I don't want you to think I'm not concerned or upset about the tragedy," Samira said. "Have you made any progress?" Her hand fiddled with the stem of the glass as she watched Nancy. "The sheriff hasn't. He was around asking me the same questions again. Maybe he thought he'd trip me up." She sighed. "I do miss her, you know." A tentative smile crossed her face. "Sure is quiet around the apartment now."

"It must be hard staying there," said Nancy. "The place has to be full of memories."

"Harder not knowing what happened to her." Samira brushed a tear away from her eye. "Why would anyone kill her? She was retired. No harm to anyone."

"I liked her too," said Nancy. "I think the answer to that question lies in what Betts did the day and evening before she was shot. Can you fill me in?"

Samira rested her chin on a hand. "I'll try to remember. Let's see. . . ." Her eyes stared thoughtfully at the pub bar. "We got up and had breakfast same as usual. Then I had my aerobics class, and Betts said she had to look up something on the computer."

The computer could have provided an answer, but too late now. Had the sheriff been in time to check the history cache? Did he even think of doing that? Now the cache had been erased, and the family had the computer. Nancy felt a twinge of disappointment. She was going to have to do some fence-mending with the sheriff. She sipped her wine and peered at Samira over the glass. "Then what happened?"

"I came back and she was gone. Then I played tennis all afternoon, so I didn't see Betts until we changed for dinner. Didn't say much to each other, but I could tell Betts had something on her mind." Samira gazed off at the landscape outside the wide windows.

"She didn't say anything?"

Samira shook her head. "Not what was on her mind. She went off to have dinner. I thought she was dining with Grace and a couple of other friends, but I didn't see her in the dining room. Anyway, I was busy with my own friends." She looked at Nancy with a twinkle in her eye. "I told you about Betts knowing the secret of Grace's old clock."

A tantalizing bit of information. Nancy nodded. "But you don't know what that was." If Betts knew the secret, at least it showed there was one, which Nancy had begun to doubt.

Samira shrugged. "She refused to say anything more about it, but she brought it up again that evening and went out the door laughing." Samira's smile faded. "And that's the last I saw of her."

"She thought of Grace as one of her friends, didn't she?" Nancy said. "Why didn't she tell Grace?"

Samira sat back and twiddled the wine glass. "Because of that bigoted cousin of hers, I expect."

Her racist, greedy cousin Jefferson. Once Betts told Grace, Jefferson would be the next to know. Nancy could see why Betts wouldn't give him the satisfaction. Anyway, secret or no secret, the clock was just a side issue. "Who else did Betts see a lot of here?" Nancy made her voice casual and looked for evasion.

"She had some former CIA buddies here. Bud and his wife Pat Grimes. Don't know the others, but they would."

"Betts worked for the CIA?" That opened up a whole new field of possibilities. Maybe Betts spotted a former spy here. This was an intriguing possibility.

"She had an unusual career path," said Samira, looking up as their food came. The server set their BLTs in front of them and withdrew.

"What do you mean?"

"Just. . .unusual. They make great sandwiches here, don't they?" Samira bit into hers.

Nancy thoughtfully ate her own sandwich, realizing that she would have to be content with Samira's meager crumbs of information. She'd interview Bud and Pat Grimes next.

"So then after dinner, what did you do?" she asked.

"Back to the apartment. I watched TV for awhile, then I went to bed. I didn't hear Betts come in if she did. Didn't think much of it at the time, since Betts liked to walk late at night. Those long dim halls are too spooky for me."

Nancy nodded. She also took late-night walks through the halls when depressing thoughts kept her awake. Even though she knew people slept behind the doors she passed and the security guard patrolled the grounds, the quiet, deserted, dimly lit halls were downright creepy. Even so, occasionally she'd hear a murmur or burst of laughter from members of the Insomniac Club playing cards in the card room.

So the last time Samira saw Betts was just before they left for dinner. She could have been captured and murdered any time after that. Nancy took a last sip of wine. Almost everyone showed up at dinner time, between five and seven. The coast would be clear then, so if Betts had suspicions about anyone, that would be the time she'd choose to break into their apartment. Considering Betts' past, is that what she would have done?

***

Nancy called Bud and Pat Grimes and set up an interview for three that afternoon. She was prompt and they ushered her into their apartment with welcoming smiles and charming grace. She sat in their living room and marveled at the display of tasteful, unusual, and probably expensive souvenirs from around the world. The coffee table itself was an elaborately carved mahogany sculpture under a square sheet of glass. Both the Grimes looked trim and fit and wore matching gray sweat pants and purple T-shirts.

"We just made some Ethiopian coffee. Would you like a cup?" Pat Grimes called back to Nancy as she headed for the kitchen.

Bud sat, legs crossed, in a massive recliner. "Fair trade coffee from the birthplace of coffee itself," he said. "You'll like it."

Pat brought in the steaming cups on a tray with cream and sugar. "We'll dispense with the ceremony, though. I can't pour coffee with the élan and spill-proof accuracy the way the Ethiopians can."

"Thank you," said Nancy. Ethiopian coffee seemed to be popular among this crowd. She already liked Bud and Pat Grimes.

"So you came to see us about Betts?" said Bud.

"Yes. You were close friends, weren't you? Colleagues?" Nancy cast another glance around the room. Had Betts traveled as much as this couple? Had she brought back from Africa all those curios in her apartment? Nancy had assumed they'd been some decorator's choice.

"We were, for awhile, but Betts tired of traveling," said Pat over her cup. "She was more interested in domestic crime and took a position over at the Department of Justice."

"Till she retired," added Bud. "We'd kept in touch over the years and when she moved here, we followed."

"We like it here," said Pat. "We travel a lot and know that when we return, everything will be just the way we left it. No worries." She smiled at Bud who winked back at her.

A lovely relationship, thought Nancy as a memory of Bill crossed her mind. Theirs, too, had been a lovely relationship. For the most part. The coffee was strong. Nancy added a dollop of cream. She needed to stay focused, but for a moment, a trace of envy had surfaced.

She leaned forward. "I think Betts found out something the day or evening before she was killed and what she learned led to her death. Did you see her at all during that time?"

"No, we didn't, but I agree," said Pat, nodding. "Consumer fraud was her special interest, you know, and there is a lot of it going on here. We've heard people talking and we went to the presentation. We even filled out the survey, but we haven't been targeted."

"Afraid of us, I expect," added Bill. "CIA and all."

Pat glanced at him, smiling. "Don't want to mess with us."

Nancy smiled too. "I'm sure that's right, but who knows you used to be in the CIA?"

Bud shrugged. "Anyone who knows us, I guess. No secret. Our bios are in the residents' directories."

"Do you think Betts suspected anyone?"

Bud and Pat looked at each other. "Not yet. She just hinted that she was on the track of something big, but we hadn't spent time alone with her for awhile. Always someone else around, so she just kept mum."

"If we'd only made time for her that day," said Pat, shaking her head. "She might still be with us."

"As for what she was doing the day or evening before, I didn't see her, except in passing." Bud looked at his wife.

"Neither did I. That was the day I took the bus into Charleston to go shopping. Betts hated that kind of excursion." Pat threw up her hands with a rueful shake of the head. "We can't help you at all."

Another dead end. Nancy put down the cup. "What about her other friends. Who were they?"

Pat shook her head and glanced at Bud. "I don't know. Maybe someone in the African-American community here. Her roommate Samira. She liked her neighbors, especially Ruth Smith."

"We're all busy here, you know," added Bud. "We know a lot of people casually through the clubs and activities, the pool and the gym, the dining hall, but really close friends? I guess that's what we were. I can't think of anyone else."

"Betts was a nice person She didn't deserve to be murdered." Pat set down her cup. "Most of the time, we'd say leave that kind of thing to the professionals. They're trained and have access to resources like criminal databases and such. But this sheriff," Pat shook her head, "I don't think he has any training at all. We don't have much hope for him solving the murders."

"Yeah," said Bud. "So we'd like to help you find her murderer." He winked at Pat. "We do have some investigation skills."

***

Nancy felt buoyed and optimistic after meeting with the Grimes. In that mood, she returned to her apartment. Malone ran to her as she entered and rubbed his body against her slacks, purring. He seemed to be back to his old self, maybe a little chastened, maybe a bit more loving after his brush with death. Nancy stroked his back, murmuring, "Nice kitty, nice kitty."

He was glad to see her, and that warmed her heart. She spent a few minutes petting and talking to him in her lap. Then she set the cat down and gazed out at the landscaped lawn and the woods beyond, thinking how much Bill had loved this cat. Her thoughts shifted and her mood darkened. Did she want to meet her newfound stepdaughter or not? The letter had already made her question everything she had thought about Bill and their relationship. Would meeting her stepdaughter change her?

Change. The word galvanized Nancy. She had never been afraid of change. She prided herself on opening doors to find out what was on the other side. If she did not, she would always wonder. And that's how she guided her life. Exploration. Adventure. Change.

She had found nothing questionable in an Internet database search. Ariana's family was well-established in a prosperous suburb of Washington, D.C. Her mother worked as a nurse for a pediatrician and her father had been a certified public accountant. He had died only a year ago, quite respectably, of a heart attack. The whole family had a blameless background, it seemed. No red flags. Whatever Nancy was afraid of lay in her own feelings and perceptions, and it had to be met full on.

She sat down at the desk, pulled out a sheet of stationery, and began a letter. She was beginning to look forward to meeting Ariana. She invited Ariana to come down for lunch, folded the letter, stamped it, and, before she could change her mind, walked briskly down the hall to the mailbox in the lobby. She hesitated a moment but then dropped the letter in the slot.

It's done now, she thought. Out of my hands. We'll see what happens next.

***

Federal Retirees Luncheon

The Association for Retired Federal Employees at Whisperwood will hold its quarterly luncheon in the private dining room at noon on Thursday.

All retired federal employees are invited to attend for this enjoyable social event. Cost: $20 per person. RSVP required. Call Pat Grimes, 555-2224.

- *The Whisperwood Breeze, Newsletter for Whisperwood Retirement Village*

Chapter 29

Grace's young nephew was leaving her apartment with a manila folder as Nancy passed by. She greeted him and turned to watch him saunter down the hall. He looked back and grinned at her. She remembered those arrogant grins, the bravado of young miscreants daring her to confront them. Was Grace even at home or did he break in?

Nancy tried the door to Grace's apartment. He'd left it locked. She peered closely at the door knob and lock. No scratches around the lock. Apparently he hadn't broken in. Nancy knocked. Footsteps approached from the other side, the door opened, and Grace stood there, startled.

"Nancy! I thought my nephew had forgotten something. I swear, he'd forget his head if it weren't fastened on." She smiled at Nancy. "Come on in."

Nancy waved her hand and stepped back. "Oh no, I saw that young man come out of your apartment. Thought he might have been up to something."

Grace laughed. "Of course not. He was just visiting, that's all. You've met him. He's my nephew."

"Of course. I'm so sorry to bother you." Nancy turned to leave.

"Not at all. Glad you're on the lookout." Grace laughed again. "See you later." She closed the door, and Nancy continued walking toward her apartment. It looked to her as if Grace's nephew had been up to mischief, but Grace knew him and had been at home, so she must have known what he took out with him.

What a suspicious mind she had, Nancy chided herself. Most of the people here had visiting grandsons, granddaughters, nieces, nephews, sons, daughters. Even she would soon have a visiting stepdaughter. Surely whoever played the part of a grandson seeking funds to get out of a Mexican jail would not show up here. With cell phones and computers, he could be anywhere in the world.

***

Rummaging through her kitchen catch-all drawer of odds and ends, Nancy pulled out the bug detector she'd used in chasing down criminals the year before. With Betts' murder and her own reputation, she thought she ought to check, just out of idle curiosity. Should have done it right after the break-in. She turned the device on and walked through her apartment. The device directed her to the land line phone in the living room. She picked up the phone and its stand, and examined them. Yes, the detector was on target. For a moment, she stared at the bug, flabbergasted. Then she probed at the tiny listening device under the phone cradle. She used to unscrew the speaker or the ear piece to look for a device but her current phone was designed differently. She began to pull it out, but stopped. She could leave it in and make use of it. Prepare a script for her and Louise that might scare the eavesdropper enough to reveal who he was. She'd have to warn the others, though.

Now on the alert, Nancy examined the furniture, lamps, vases, bed, and other pieces of furniture for another bug. She found a tiny video camera high on the wall in her bedroom and another in her bathroom. She could imagine what use might be made of those videos and shivered as she knocked them down with a broom handle and then crushed them with her foot.

So that's why the break-in. Not to steal but to place the bug and cameras. How interesting. No. Nancy amended that. For the video cameras, how contemptible. So contemptible that Nancy rethought her earlier decision and pried the bug out of the phone. She pulled pliers out of the kitchen drawer and crushed the bug. She picked up the crushed cameras and threw them all in the waste basket. Then she scrubbed her hands to remove the filth of such low tactics. She ran a final sweep of her apartment, then put the bug detector away. "Got them all," she thought. Nothing she did in the privacy of her apartment would lend itself to blackmail, but someone else might be more vulnerable. Someone who resorted to consumer fraud and murder wouldn't stop at blackmail.

Home Services for All
Those Chores You Hate

> Whisperwood's Home Services include cleaning, rug shampooing, picture hanging, dry cleaning, even pet sitting, and a multitude of other chores to help make your life at Whisperwood easier and more enjoyable. Whatever you need, call Bev at Home Services to find out more and to schedule a service. 555-6612.
>
> *- The Whisperwood Breeze, Newsletter for Whisperwood Retirement Village.*

Chapter 30

Rain poured down outside, drenching the spring daffodils and new green buds on the trees. Nancy had walked up the stairs from the first floor to the sixth floor twice and the length of the building once to make up for the usual mile-long walk she couldn't take today because of the rain. She needed that walk desperately to work out the kinks, give her perspective, keep her optimistic. Right now, she needed that optimism. After today, she didn't think her life would ever be the same.

She sighed. The clock said ten-thirty. Her new-found stepdaughter was driving down from Morgantown to meet her at eleven. Then they were going to have lunch in the dining room. What would this young woman be like? Nancy envisioned a blonde prom queen, all bubbly personality. How could she bear it?

Yet as she thought about it, she realized that in her young days, people might have thought of her as a blonde prom queen. Bubbly personality? She sighed. Probably. That's what they would have thought.

She apologized to Malone as she enticed him into the bedroom with a treat and closed the door on him. She didn't need him freaking out today, too.

She took a quick look at her living room, at the clutter and the dust, then closed the door and walked with leaden feet down the hall to the lobby and her doom.

The two Rottweilers, Ham and Eggs, greeted her as she entered the lobby. Some kind soul had brought them in out of the rain. They were clean and dry. Nancy knelt down to hug first one, then the other, feeling comforted by their effusive tail-wagging and enthusiastic kisses. Dogs weren't complicated. They loved you and showed it.

Louise's table was still set up, but she wasn't there. She only needed a few more signatures on her petition. Nancy passed by on her way to look out the double glass entrance doors.

The dogs sat at her feet as she watched a young woman fighting with a beige umbrella walk toward her from the parking lot. Could she be wearing a trench coat? Nancy almost smiled. The young woman—this must be Ariana—paused under the portico to shake out her umbrella and close it. To Nancy, it seemed as if Ariana deliberately did not look up to greet the woman waiting for her. Maybe, like Nancy, she was also seeking to put off an awkward moment.

Her hair was dark brown, and she was tall, almost six feet, it seemed to Nancy. She seemed to be taking an inordinately long time with the umbrella. Finally, Nancy walked out under the portico to meet her. "Are you Ariana?"

She looked at Nancy for the first time and smiled. Nancy saw that her eyes were brown, like Bill's. They sparkled. She extended her hand. "I am. And you're Ms. Dickenson?"

There was something so open about her smile that Nancy's heart warmed. "I am, but please call me Nancy."

"Thank you. I am so thrilled to meet you." Ariana giggled. "How do you like my costume?"

Nancy's eyes swept down Ariana's figure, covered by the trench coat. "Costume?"

"Oh well. I guess it's a dud." She giggled again. "I thought that since you were a famous detective, I'd dress the part for you. Only without a deerstalker hat and pipe. Was that a bad idea?"

Nancy laughed. "I get it. The trench coat. I did wonder. . ." The girl was delightful. All Nancy's misgivings disappeared like nightmares in the morning. "Come on in." She walked back through the automatic glass doors. Ariana followed behind.

"I thought we'd go to my apartment first," said Nancy. "I have photos of Bill—your father, that is—and memorabilia. You might like going through them, then we'll go to lunch."

"Great! Can I meet Malone too?" Ariana's long stride swept her down the hall ahead of Nancy, who found it difficult to keep up, until Ariana turned to her.

"Oops. I forgot. Everyone complains I walk too fast." She slowed her pace.

"I'm usually a fast walker too," Nancy said, "but you've got me beat. You know about Malone?"

"Oh yes," said Ariana. "I wanted to know about my birth father." She looked at Nancy. "After I found out about him, that is. I uncovered some old reviews and articles online about his magician act. They mentioned Malone." She paused, staring down at her hands. "You must think it awfully pushy of me to come see you."

Nancy didn't know what to say, since that had been exactly what she thought, but they reached the apartment. Ariana paused at the hall shelf, her eyes focused on the photos Nancy had placed there that morning. One was a wedding portrait; the other was a group photo. Now Nancy wondered what had possessed her to do that, some kind of possessiveness? Wanting to assert her own relationship with Bill? How odd of her. "Yes, that's our wedding picture and the other one is of us, a year before he died. That's Malone we're holding."

Ariana studied the pictures. "Mom doesn't have any pictures of him."

Nancy opened the door and stepped inside. Ariana tore her eyes away from the wedding photo and followed Nancy into the apartment.

"You've had a long drive. Would you like a soft drink or hot tea?" Nancy knew she did.

Ariana was glancing around the apartment. "A Coke?"

"Sure." Nancy brought out two glasses of Coke and a plate of cookies. She sat on one end of the couch, Ariana on the other. "So tell me about yourself," Nancy said.

Ariana smiled at Nancy and took her hands in both of hers. "Here's the deal. My father died a year ago—that is, the father I grew up with. My real father. When I went off to college, my mother decided I should learn the truth, so she wrote me a letter. It must have been very hard for her to do because she didn't give it to me until I started my junior year in college. I guess she was worried about how I'd take it, and it took some getting used to, I can tell you.

"And then it took me a while to get up the nerve to write you, but I want to know about my birth father. Who was he? What was he like? I didn't even know what he looked like." She stopped and waited for Nancy to respond.

Nancy cleared her throat. The way Ariana spoke, her gestures, even the quirky smile reminded her so much of Bill. She managed to ask, "May I see your mother's letter?"

Ariana nodded, squeezing Nancy's hand as if she understood all that Nancy was feeling. A perceptive young lady.

"Of course. I did bring it." Ariana rummaged in her purse and pulled out a letter that was creased and torn as if it had been read many times. "I will be glad to share the letter with you, if you care to read it. Can I tell you the gist of it, though?"

Nancy felt stunned. This girl was full of bombshells. "Just a minute," she gasped. "I need to catch my breath."

"Are you all right?" Ariana asked.

Nancy took a deep breath and managed to say, "I'm fine." She remembered the one thing that people always said about her. Curious. Nosy, some said. And she was curious about Bill and the woman who had borne such a. . .delightful. . .child. "Give me the gist," she said. "Maybe later I'd like to read the letter."

Ariana studied her. "Good," she said. "Good. Here it is, then. You must know my, uh, birth father's first wife had been ill for several years. My mother was a nurse and tended to her. Her own husband—her first one, that is—had died just a few months before. My mother was very young and her husband had been in the military." Ariana paused and looked at Nancy as if for understanding. "I can see how it was. Two lonely people, your husband and my mother, trying to cope with grief. They took solace in one another for awhile, and my mother became pregnant with me."

"But why didn't they marry eventually?" asked Nancy. She, too, could understand the grief and the need for solace.

"I don't know," said Ariana, "but they just didn't. I asked her, though, but didn't get an answer. Probably the age difference. Anyway, my mother married someone else, and he is my real father. He was very kind and generous to me. I was very lucky. I thought he was my birth father until I read the letter." She stopped and lifted her chin. "I will always think of him as my real father."

"Of course," Nancy said.

Ariana continued. "In the end, my mother felt I had a right to know and, after all, both my birth father and my real father were dead by then, and I guess she thought I couldn't stir things up any more."

"But you have," said Nancy. "Your letter was quite a shock to me."

Ariana looked at her. "Was it? But he died awhile back and the affair was long over before he met you."

Nancy smiled. Ariana had done her research indeed. "Still, I had never known this about him. It made me wonder who he was."

Ariana opened her palms to Nancy. "He was the same man he always was."

Nancy nodded. "Yes, I think so. He was kind, intelligent, loving, imaginative, creative." She smiled at Ariana. "You would have liked his magic show."

"I know. I'm so sorry I never got to meet him." Ariana glanced around the apartment. "Where's Malone?"

At the sound of his name, Malone let out a long, loud, mournful meow. Nancy rose and walked over to her bedroom to open the door. Malone stalked out, tail high in the air, and gave Nancy a reproachful look. He sniffed at Ariana as he passed on his way to his food bowl in the kitchen.

"Wow, he's big, isn't he?" said Ariana. "Quite a character."

Nancy smiled. "As you said. Quite a character. He'll come out to greet you once he gets over his displeasure." She rose and walked to the credenza. "Would you like to see some family photos?"

Ariana clapped her hands. "Oh yes, please. I'd love to see them. I want to know everything about my, uh, father."

Ariana had trouble calling Bill her father. This was all as new to her as it was to Nancy. She warmed to the girl. A nice girl. Nancy retrieved three albums from the credenza and took them over to Ariana. "What are you studying in college?"

"Anthropology and archaeology. With a little geology thrown in.

I'll be a senior next year. Then grad school."

"What exciting fields!" Nancy was thrilled. This was an unusual girl. Anthropology and archaeology. And a little geology. Suddenly, Nancy wanted to know Ariana a lot better. Anthropology and archaeology were fields that had always thrilled her, although her tastes ran more toward Mel Fisher's sunken treasures or pirate gold. If she were to be truthful, digging in the dirt under a hot sun did not appeal to her, and potsherds were just drab little bits of clay, not gold.

Ariana's eyes glowed. "I love the field work and I'm thrilled when I find a piece of pottery someone made centuries ago. I plan to go on for advanced degrees in archaeology."

Her enthusiasm made Nancy smile. She surprised herself by saying, "I hope you'll keep me posted on what you do. I'm fascinated by archaeology."

"Are you? Of course I'll let you know." Her attention turned to the albums. She picked up the top one and opened it. Nancy began to point out the photos and tell Bill's daughter about her father. The time passed with both of them absorbed in the albums. Nancy's heart warmed even more to Ariana. The dread had dissipated as Nancy thought about her own loneliness and depression as she nursed her first husband through his final illness and then, much later, Bill. She had not found someone to offer her solace and companionship during those dark days. What would she have done if she had? She could not blame Bill and certainly not his daughter.

As Ariana pored over the photos, Nancy studied her, seeking out those features that reminded her of Bill. The eyes for sure. Her enthusiasm. Her imagination.

Nancy looked up from her musings and glanced at the clock. Good heavens! It was one o'clock. They'd been there for two hours.

"I promised you lunch," Nancy said. "I'm hungry, aren't you?"

Ariana laughed. "I guess I am. Forgot about lunch. Thank you so much for sharing these photos with me."

Nancy rose. "We can come back to them after lunch if you'd like."

Ariana glanced at her watch. "I'll have to be getting back to Morgantown by then. But maybe I can come back?" She followed Nancy out the door into the hall. "If that would be all right?"

Nancy smiled at her. "Of course. You can come anytime you like." Then Nancy surprised herself by adding, "And perhaps, someday you can bring your mother too."

Ariana shrugged. "I'll see." She looked up at Nancy. "Oh! I didn't mean that the way it sounded. My mother would like to meet you." Ariana reached over to lay a hand on Nancy's arm. "She told me to tell you that Bill never knew she was pregnant. She didn't let him know because she was not right for him, and she knew he wasn't right for her. Odd, isn't it?"

Nancy could feel the tears pricking at her eyelids. Ariana was so young. How could she know that those words would be such a comfort? Bill never knew, and so, there was no question of desertion or any of those ugly thoughts that had surfaced since she had first received the letter.

They entered the dining room and Nancy relaxed. They spent a pleasant hour with Nancy sharing episodes from her career and Ariana telling Nancy about her college life.

As they walked to the lobby after lunch, Nancy added, "I hope you will visit me again. And let me know how things are going for you."

"Thank you," said Ariana. "I'd like that."

***

Welcome Our Returning College Students

Plan now to welcome back our returning college students and scholarship recipients. May 25, 4 to 5:30 p.m. in the Pub. Refreshments will be served. They'll be eager to tell you about their studies and career plans. Most will be working at Whisperwood over the summer to fill in for vacationing staff.

- *The Whisperwood Breeze, Newsletter for Whisperwood Retirement Village*

CHAPTER 31

The rain had stopped. Nancy walked out to Ariana's car with her and waved good-bye as Ariana headed down the mountain. Upon returning to the lobby, Nancy stood by as Louise, clipboard in hand, snagged another passerby. She winked at Nancy while the man signed the petition. Louise thanked him and then walked over to Nancy.

"How did it go?" she asked.

"Fine." Nancy grinned. "I like her. Ariana is intelligent, interesting, and quite nice."

"Saw you pass by." Louise nodded. "You look relieved. Glad to hear it."

Nancy checked her watch. "Can you join me for an hour or so around four-thirty?"

"Sure. I've got all the signatures I need." She waved her clipboard. "We'll get this passed now."

"Good. I'll meet you back here in the lobby then. Four-thirty. Dress inconspicuously and bring a spade and cutting shears."

Louise raised an eyebrow. "I'm not going to get my wrist broken again, am I?"

"We're just going on a little sightseeing expedition, that's all."

Nancy patted Louise on the back as she left. "I'll tell you when I see you."

Louise was waiting for Nancy promptly at four-thirty, and they headed out the front entrance. Nancy had changed into jeans and a blue cotton shirt. She carried a bucket, hand towel, and clipboard. Louise wore tan slacks and green shirt and carried a spade. "This is as inconspicuous as I get," she said. "Couldn't find shears. What's up?"

"Let's go out to the bench by the tennis courts, and I'll explain." Nancy led the way. No one was on the courts since the dinner hour was approaching. The sun was still high, but this was the time when most residents were either congregating outside the dining room or sipping a pre-dinner cocktail at the pub.

She dried off the bench with the towel before sitting on it. Louise plopped down beside her. From where they sat, the yellow crime scene tape was just visible. Nancy pointed it out to Louise.

"Yeah. I can see it from my apartment," Louise said. "A lot of shrubbery there. Probably why they chose that spot."

"When Betts was murdered, she must have gone out—or been taken out—one of the back doorways," Nancy said, shooing away a bee.

"Hey, be careful. That's one of my girls you're hitting," Louise said.

"Sorry." Nancy wiped off her hands with the towel. "Or she left by a ground floor terrace apartment along the rear of the building."

"I get it. We'll go alongside the rear, pretending to study the landscaping there, but really. . ."

"Really we'll be looking for any clues to how and where Betts left the building." Nancy said. "Once we know that, we might have a clue about why, how, or when she was killed."

"It rained all morning," Louise said.

"I should have thought of doing this earlier." Nancy agreed. "I presume the sheriff has been all over the ground looking for clues. I'm just trying to spot possibilities. It's one thing to note all the clues. It takes a bit of imagination to interpret them."

"Sheriff seems like a linear thinker to me with a limit on imagination." Louise stood, brushing off the seat of her pants. "Look for anything odd in the apartments, too. We can get pretty close pretending to examine the plants."

Nancy took off for the back of the building. "Of course."

Their charade played well although the audience was virtually nonexistent. As Nancy surmised, most of the residents were gathering for dinner. Since many of them left a light on in their apartments, Nancy and Louise could peek through the windows as they pretended to study the landscaping. They saw only one or two people left in the rooms.

"What a dull lot," said Louise. "Aside for a few unusual souvenirs, most of these apartments show no imagination." She whistled. "Look at this, Nancy. She tugged Nancy toward a bedroom window. "This is Stag Williams' apartment. He's calmed down in the last year, but he used to plague all of us women with his so-called attentions."

Nancy peered through the glass. A huge canopied bed with red netting and tassels dominated the room. "Are those lava lamps?" asked Nancy.

Louise snorted. "Haven't seen them since the seventies."

"Move on, Louise," Nancy said. "We're not here to pry." She moved closer to Grace's apartment. Was Grace what she seemed? The door to the second bedroom had always been closed when Nancy was there. She wondered. . . .

She snuck up to Grace's terrace and looked through the glass doors in time to see Grace leave. No lights left on, and the terrace was bare of plants and ornaments. The second bedroom was on the right. Nancy crept up to that window. The shade was drawn, leaving only a couple of inches at the bottom to peer through. Nancy squinted and shaded her eyes as she peered into the room. A computer screen on a long table had been left on and lent additional light to the scene. Except for the table and chairs, the room was bare, but it looked like a business office. They could see several cell phones also lying on the table

"Ever hear of Grace having any kind of business?" whispered Nancy.

Louise had crept over and looked through the window with Nancy. "That stuff looks serious. What's going on there?" She glanced at Nancy. Nancy knew she was remembering the thefts and murders that had terrified Whisperwood the year before. "Could be her husband has some kind of business. Maybe a dot-com," Louise said.

"She's never mentioned anything about it. She would if it were legitimate."

"And making money," added Louise. "If not, it would be an embarrassment."

"We need to find out what is going on there." Nancy crept onto the terrace. "Right now while she's at dinner." She tried the terrace door. "Locked."

"I'm starting to have a bad feeling about this." Louise backed away from the windows. She and Nancy returned to the path and entered the building at the side entrance.

"Just a minute." Nancy disappeared in her apartment and returned a minute later, dangling a set of tools. "My lock picks. We need to get in and out fast."

"A really bad feeling." Louise shook her head. "This is how we got into trouble the last time."

Nancy opened the lock to Grace's door and slipped inside. Louise hesitated, but Nancy pulled her in. She headed for the second bedroom. The door was locked. The picks came into play again. Nancy opened the door and stepped inside.

"It looks like a phone bank," said Louise, stepping across the tangle of wires on the floor. Nancy scanned through the papers on the long business-like table. She held up one of the papers. "This one has notes about you and me." Nancy read through the text. "She lists probable income." Nancy looked up with a grin. "Got it way off base for me, but she does include a note saying I have no close relatives."

"Let me see that." Louise grabbed the paper and squinted at it through her glasses. "Pretty close on my income." Louise's tone turned indignant. "And she has stuff here about my daughter."

She read through the papers. "Estimates of income, hobbies, activities. . ." Nancy looked at Louise. "This is downright creepy."

Louise rubbed her wrist. "Let's get out of here, Nancy." She headed for the hall door. Nancy followed. They stopped as the door slowly opened, and Grace entered.

She gaped at them. "Nancy! Louise! What are you doing here?" Her eyes moved beyond Nancy to the open door of the second bedroom.

They stared at each other for a moment. Nancy could think of nothing to say that would explain a legitimate reason for being in Grace's apartment.

Louise made an attempt. "We, uh, smelled smoke and thought there was a fire in here. We're all nervous after the auditorium fire."

"Looks like you're running a business here," Nancy began, pasting on a smile and keeping her tone light.

Grace narrowed her eyes, drew herself up and snorted. "You're lying. You've been snooping. You have no business being here and looking into our things. You're worse than that nuisance Betts." She reached into her purse and pulled out a gun. "Betts was nosy too."

She waved the gun at them. "Stay right where you are," she said.

***

No Guns Allowed

No firearms of any type except those carried by security personnel are permitted on the Whisperwood campus at any time. This is to ensure everyone's safety. We don't need to remind you of the statistics, but the fact is that firearms in the home lead to homicide, whether accidental or not.

You may turn your weapons in to the sheriff at his office, no questions asked. For only a small fee, Mike's Sporting Goods store on Main Street in town will store your hunting rifles and make sure they are in top condition when hunting season starts. He will also take your guns in trade.

Whisperwood's Security Personnel handle all safety concerns.

- Notice from the Whisperwood Residents Committee

CHAPTER 32

Grace glared at Nancy and Louise through narrowed eyes. She pushed her lips in and out as if she were deciding what to do with the two trespassers. The way she waved the gun from Nancy to Louise showed she meant business. She seemed to make a decision. "Get down on the floor, hands behind you," she barked at them.

Nancy glanced at Louise, who was eying Grace as if she planned to attack. Nancy reached out a restraining hand and stared beyond Grace moving her mouth as if she were silently giving instructions to someone behind Grace.

Grace was not to be fooled. She aimed the gun at Nancy, then at Louise. "I said down on the floor. Now!" She backed away from them. "I said now," she repeated, menace in her voice. She reached behind her to the tasseled drapery rope and drew the drapes across the doors to the terrace.

Nancy reached over to help Louise. This is all my fault, Nancy thought. I've gotten Louise into another dangerous situation. Nancy glanced at Louise's white face. The pain in her wrist, broken the summer before, must be agonizing. Nancy helped Louise down to the floor, feeling Grace's eyes watching every move.

"I have to help Louise," Nancy said, making her voice quaver.

"She can't get down easily. Her wrist still hasn't healed fully."

"I don't care. Just get down." Grace stepped to the phone as she watched Nancy put an arm around Louise. Nancy wasn't sure how this gambit might help, but it slowed the pace and made Grace nervous.

"I'm all right," Louise whispered.

"You heard her," Grace said. She prodded Nancy with her foot. "Get down on the floor."

Nancy complied, seeing no way to avoid it.

Closing the draperies made the room dim and shadowy. Could they use that?

Nancy stared at Louise sending a message with her eyes. *Look for anything that will serve as a weapon.* Louise nodded.

The gun didn't have a silencer. If Grace used it, would anyone hear the gunshot? Nancy answered her own question. No, they wouldn't. The apartments were well-constructed with reinforced concrete floors and walls. Someone immediately outside the hall door might hear the gunshot, but would they recognize it as such or think of it as something on television? Probably they would pass by without a thought. And right now, everyone was at dinner. Even Fitz and George. Would they miss Nancy and Louise? Would they launch a search? They would wonder what happened. They might call or stop by the apartments. Finding no one, would they check the parking lot for her car?

Nancy thought Fitz and George would start searching, but in a low-key way. They might stop by Grace's apartment, but she could easily send them away. She could even invent a spurious errand for Nancy and Louise. Say they'd taken the shuttle to some event in town. Be vague enough so whatever happened, she would be in the clear. Nancy heard Louise groan. *I should never have made Louise come in with me. Whatever happens will be my fault.*

Grace picked up a cell phone and tapped in a number. "Get down," she repeated, prodding Nancy with her foot. Nancy stalled as if she couldn't bend easily, gradually resting her knees on the floor, but keeping her eyes level with the coffee table top. A hard-bound library book lay there.

Grace kept the gun aimed at Nancy, but her attention was on the phone.

Nancy raised an eyebrow at Louise who nodded. In one swift movement, Nancy picked up the book and hurled it at Grace.

Grace shrieked and ducked. Nancy pulled Louise up and flew forward to attack Grace. Louise went for the gun.

As they wrestled, a voice yelled, "Stop right there."

All three froze and turned toward the door. Grace's husband Richard stood in the doorway. He pulled the door shut behind him. He drew a small gun out of the briefcase he carried and pointed it at Nancy. "Get away from her, now!"

Nancy let go of Grace. Louise stepped back and began rubbing her wrist. Freed from their attack and protected by Richard, Grace slashed out with her gun hand at Louise and then Nancy. Her rage grew as she pummeled them with the gun while Nancy and Louise shielded their heads and bodies with their arms.

"Stop it!" yelled Richard in a booming voice that commanded attention. Grace looked at him and stopped. She stepped away from Nancy and Louise, nursing her hand. "They started it," she said with a pout. She sounded like a three-year-old. Nancy almost laughed at the absurdity.

"All right. What happened?" Richard asked, looking from Nancy to Louise to Grace.

"I was trying to call you," Grace said, still nursing her gun hand. "They know what's going on. We've got to get rid of them." She walked away from Nancy and Louise to stand beside Richard.

"Wait a minute." Richard stepped away from Grace and toward the door. "I didn't sign on for no killings."

"Oh yeah?" Grace sneered. "Did you forget about Betts? You're in it now, Buddy Boy, and don't you forget it. We've got to get rid of these two. We took care of one nosy bitch. Two more won't make a difference."

Nancy begged to differ. She glanced at Louise. Could they possibly bargain with this man for their lives? "Grace is a murderer," Nancy said. "She'll be caught and punished. If you have nothing to do with her, you can escape. At least you won't be charged with murder." Actually he would be but now was not the time to quibble.

"We won't be caught," Grace said. "We've got a good thing going here, and you two busybodies are not going to mess it up." She walked over to stand beside her husband. She put her arm through his and looked up at him. "We're making good money here. More than you'd see in a lifetime anywhere else. It's a sweet set-up. This isn't the time to give it up."

"I don't like it," said Richard, disengaging her arm. "If these two found us, it won't be long 'fore the sheriff is onto us. A murder rap is bad stuff."

"We're not the only ones who know about you," said Louise.

Nancy nodded. "We're not. The other 90s Club members know about you too. They know we came to see you, and they're waiting to hear what we found out."

Too late Nancy realized she had just put George and Fitz in danger.

Grace put her hands on her hips, the gun dangling from one hand, and contemplated first Nancy, then Louise, frowning as she pushed her lips in and out. Richard looked nervous and his gun wavered from one to the other as he waited for Grace to speak.

"I didn't bargain for this," he finally said. "I'm outta here." He dropped the gun in his briefcase and turned to leave.

"No!" Grace yelled. "Get back here. I need you to help me get rid of them. Then you can leave, but you'll be cutting yourself out of a lot of green and a good life."

Richard stopped on the way to the door. "I don't think so," he said. "I'm not into any killing of nobody. We're just running scams here. That's all. No rough stuff. You had to go and kill that girl."

Grace licked her lips. "We've got ninety-five thousand dollars cash so far out of this set-up. You can have it all if you help me. If you don't, I'll make sure the cops get you for murdering all three."

Nancy and Louise watched spellbound at this negotiation. Richard hesitated, glanced over at the gun in Grace's hand, then at the gun in his own. "We can't get rid of them here," he said. They've got to disappear somewhere else, then no one can connect us with them. Maybe they can just disappear altogether so no one finds them. No bodies, no murders."

A look of triumph crossed Grace's face. "Of course they've got to disappear," she said, her voice becoming softly persuasive. "Then you'll get your money, and we can disappear too. No one will ever know. Thanks to their butting in, this place is played out."

"You don't have to kill us," said Nancy. "You're going to disappear anyway. All you have to do is change your appearance and your names and you'll get clean away."

Richard nodded. "She's right. We don't have to kill nobody. You just give me my money and I'm outta here. You're outta here. People may not even believe them, whatever they say."

Grace walked over to Richard and with one quick motion, ripped the briefcase out of his hand. "Are you that dumb? You think you can ever walk down a street again without worrying someone will recognize you? We let these two go free, and you'll risk being picked up every time you show yourself."

"Not if you change your appearance," said Nancy. "You wouldn't even have to do much." She looked at Richard. "Especially you. Get a crew cut and no one will ever see you as the same man again. You'll be clear. Let Grace take care of herself."

"Yeah," added Louise. "And crew cuts are easy to manage, too." She flicked her long, gray braid.

Grace snickered. "You two are a bunch of jokers, aren't you?" She kept her eyes on Nancy and Louise, while saying to Richard. "Help me tie them up. We've got to wait till late tonight, like before, to get them out of here."

Like before? Nancy thought. That's what they did with Betts. Betts was snooping and got caught just like she and Louise.

Grace waved the gun at Nancy and Louise. "Get down on the floor. This time I mean it. No funny business. Keep your hands on the floor above your heads."

Once both Nancy and Louise were stretched out on the floor, Grace turned to Richard. "Get moving, will you? Find the duct tape."

Duct tape. Nancy glanced at Louise.

"Phooey," Louise muttered. "Duct tape."

Nancy's heart sank too. She knew how to deal with rope. Duct tape was another proposition. They'd been tied up with duct tape before. If she ever got out of this alive, Nancy swore that she would never buy another roll of it. Too many bad memories.

She watched Richard hesitate and Grace rush in to persuade. "I'll tell you what. You help me get these two into my car, and you don't have to do nothing more, okay? You get half the ninety-five thousand and leave. You won't be involved in any murders. We'll make these two disappear so there won't be any murder rap hanging over us, and you'll be scot-free. No bodies. No murders."

"I don't know. . ." Richard hesitated, as he looked down at

Nancy and Louise, shaking his head.

"Come on. Let's go." Grace waved the gun. "The sooner you help me with this, the sooner you can get outta here."

Still shaking his head, Richard said, "Okay. I want the money and I want to get away from this place."

"Don't forget all the money we've got tied up in a deposit on this place." Grace kicked Nancy in the leg. "This would have been a sweet set-up if we'd been left alone."

"That's right," Richard said, rubbing his chin.

"Sure. Now get the duct tape out of the closet." She nodded toward the linen closet. "Let's put these two out of commission." She sat in one of the wicker chairs and set her shoe down hard on Nancy's ankle. Nancy winced. "I'm got my eye on both of you, so don't try any funny business."

Nancy couldn't see her watch, but it must be about five-thirty. Grace wouldn't dare move them until after ten that evening. Too many people about. Would Fitz or George look for them? Maybe. Would they think of Grace's apartment? Probably not. No one was going to help. Panic threatened to overwhelm her. With an effort, Nancy forced her thoughts toward escape. Richard didn't want to be involved in this. How could they persuade him to free them?

They'd be bound with duct tape, separately to make it easier to move them. Then they'd be carried, helpless, to the car and maybe placed in the trunk. Nancy looked around for anything that might work as a knife or sharp tool. She saw nothing on the floor that would help and there were only keys and the lock picks in her pockets. But she did have a safety pin shortening her panty's waistline. How horrified her childhood housekeeper would be. A safety pin. A modest weapon indeed, but her sloppy habits might save her life.

Richard returned with a roll of silver duct tape. "My favorite color," quipped Louise as he unwound a strip and wrapped her wrists together behind her back. Nancy saw her wince as the rough treatment hurt her fragile wrist. Then Louise's ankles were bound and a strip placed across her mouth. Nancy received the same treatment.

If only their captors would leave. Surely they'd go out to dinner, wouldn't they? Grace turned on the television and sat on the couch watching some insipid quiz show. She and Richard both glanced occasionally at their two captives, but Nancy could see they felt confident that she and Louise were totally incapacitated.

Grace knelt down by Nancy's side and rummaged in the pocket of her jeans, pulling out Nancy's keys. She dangled them in front of Nancy as she stood. She turned to Richard. "Be right back."

"Where you going?" he asked.

"Never mind." She opened the door, peered out, and left. Nancy watched her go. If only she could speak. Richard wasn't a murderer. He might let them go. Even though she mumbled through the gag, stared at him, and writhed on the floor, he ignored her. In a few minutes, that chance was lost. Grace was back, carrying the old clock, but her legs were bleeding from long scratches. "That damn cat," she said.

Good ol' Malone. Nancy glared at Grace and hoped Malone hadn't been hurt.

Grace set the clock down and disappeared into the bathroom. A few minutes later, she was back with the blood washed off. "Six p.m. I'm going to dinner," she said to Richard. "I'll bring you back something."

"Make it good," Richard muttered.

"Keep an eye on them." Grace nodded at Nancy and laughed. Nancy struggled again to get his attention. When he looked at her, she pleaded with her eyes, but he quickly turned away as if he could ignore the facts he couldn't see. Nancy struggled with the tape, but duct tape is tough stuff. Whenever she glanced at Louise, her guilt grew. Louise lay still as if any movement was too much to endure. Her face was white, and she did not open her eyes. Nancy could only imagine the pain she was in.

Grace returned at seven with a carry-out from the dining room. She handed the food to Richard and then turned to Nancy, bound and helpless on the floor.

"Met your friends," Grace said with a sneer. "Told them I saw you two go off with somebody in a car." She grinned. "And, no, didn't notice who it was or anything about the car." She turned her back and sat down on the couch to watch television.

Nancy ignored her. She could do nothing right now anyway. She had the germ of a possibility but that would have to wait until they were alone. Surely they'd be locked in a car trunk. Isn't that what murderers did? Nancy was counting on it. She dozed occasionally, but now every time she woke, she saw Louise staring at her over the duct tape. Nancy blinked several times in an attempt to reassure her, but the message was too oblique to register.

At ten, Grace clicked off the television, rose, stretched, and yawned. She grabbed Richard's shoulder and shook him awake. "I'm going to bring the car around to the back on the service road and open the trunk." She walked to the hall door. "When you see the trunk open, carry them out, one at a time."

Nancy's spirits rose. They would be placed in the trunk and driven somewhere. They had a chance to survive this evening.

"When do I get my share of the deposit and the ninety-five thousand?"

Grace glared at him from the door. "When the job is done and not before."

She opened the door and left, jangling the keys in her hand.

Richard paced the floor, glancing at Nancy and Louise now and then and muttering to himself. Nancy kept herself calm as they waited. It seemed a long time before a tap finally sounded on the terrace doors. Richard turned off the lights, opened the drapes, and peered into the darkness outside.

"About time you got here," he said as he slid the doors open. Grace stepped into the room, an unlit cigarette hanging off her lip.

"Shut up" she said.

She put her hands on her hips and eyed Nancy. "This is all your fault, you know." She turned to Richard. "I opened the trunk. Coast is clear. Get them out there fast." Grace held the drapes back and peered through the darkness at the other apartments.

Richard picked Nancy up first. He muttered "Sorry" as her head hit the door, but he carried her out and placed her gently in the trunk. At least he had some heart, Nancy thought, shifting her position. Something was digging into her back. Then he brought Louise out and stuck her in beside Nancy. Louise's eyes bulged over the gag. She was terrified. So am I, thought Nancy, but I have a plan. I have hope. She doesn't. The trunk door closed on them.

Nancy maneuvered her bound hands to reach down inside her slacks to open the safety pin and pluck it out of the waistband of her underpants. She now had a sharp point to use as a pick. She felt around in the darkness until she found Louise's wrists and used the pin to tear at the duct tape there. She knew she was hurting Louise's vulnerable wrist and tried to be gentle.

Duct tape was tough stuff, but once the tape was weakened by a tear, it could be shredded apart. Nancy could hear the tape ripping as she worked on it with the pin. Louise twisted her wrists to further weaken it until she could pull her hands apart. Louise took the pin and began using it on Nancy's wrists. Once their hands were free, they pulled off the strips across their mouths, smothering the yelps as the tape peeled off skin and hair. Then they used the pin to free their ankles. They grabbed each other's hands and shook them. Even though there were no lights in the trunk, the rear tail lights cast a reddish glow through cracks around the frame. Nancy saw Louise turn away to wipe the tears from her eyes.

Now to find out what had dug into her back. Nancy reached around for the object and pulled out a tire iron. She stifled a laugh. The perfect weapon.

They were free, and they had a weapon. They could not ask for better circumstances considering the predicament they were in. Nancy listened for any clues as to where they were going. They had traveled on a smooth road, but it was too quiet to be a highway with traffic. Nancy couldn't read her watch in the darkness even if she hadn't been busy with the pin. She guessed that they were on that road for half an hour, then the car had slowed and turned and the road became bumpy and felt rutted. A dirt road. It could be a country lane, but because of the need for secrecy, Grace had probably found an old logging trail in the woods. She had to drive slow because of the ruts but needed to go far enough to find an isolated place to dump two bodies. Nancy adjusted her arms so she could swing the tire iron when the trunk opened.

The car stopped. Nancy heard the doors open and the car sway as Grace and Richard got out on each side of the car. The doors slammed shut. She heard the crunching of sticks and leaves as they walked around to the back of the car. She felt Louise tense as Nancy brought the tire iron into position to strike. She held her breath.

"Walk over there and see if that's a good place to dump them," Grace said.

"Are you sure you want to do this?" Richard whined. "We can just leave them here, maybe even tied up. Then it won't be our fault. Maybe they won't ever be found."

Nancy heard Grace's grim laugh, then more crunching of sticks and dry leaves. "Here's a good place," she said. "Start digging."

A dubious Richard said, "You sure? Seems too close to the road."

Nancy heard the scraping of a shovel and plop of dirt, then it became rhythmic. Scrape, plop. Scrape, plop. That went on a long time.

Finally, Nancy heard Grace say, "That's good enough. Hand me the shovel." There was a gunshot and a groan, then the thud and rustle of something falling on the leaves. Grace had the gun. Had she shot Richard? Her accomplice? That meant she would not hesitate to kill them, Nancy had no doubts about that.

The sounds of scraping and plopping resumed, but soon stopped. Nancy heard Grace approach the car, but she passed the trunk and opened the driver's door, then the car swayed as she got in and started the car. Grace wasn't going to risk leaving their bodies near Richard's. Nancy felt the car move down the rutted road. Some minutes later, the car stopped again. Nancy felt Louise grip her arm as Grace approached the trunk. Then the trunk door opened.

Nancy swung the tire iron hard, first on the hand, then on the body and as the body crumpled, on the head. Grace slid to the ground. Nancy and Louise crawled out of the car. The headlights were still on, lighting the darkness around them. Grace lay slumped where she'd fallen. Blood gushed from the head wound and her hand looked broken and bruised. Nancy pried the gun out of Grace's hand and walked around to the driver's seat. The keys were still in the car. Good. "Let's get out of here."

"You said it." Louise climbed into the car. "We've got to retrace Grace's tracks on this dirt road. Can you see which way she came? Then we call the police. I don't think anything can be done for

Richard." Louise glanced back at Grace, sitting on the ground, moaning and holding her head.

"Ambulance too." How badly was Grace injured? "If we can find our way out of here." Nancy started the car and began edging backwards down the trail. She glanced in the rear view mirror. Nothing but blackness in back. "I've got to turn around." The wheels spun as Nancy slowly turned the car around and headed back the way Grace had come through the woods, following a trail made conspicuous in the headlights by the ruffled leaves and cracked twigs.

"I'm looking for signs of where we stopped before," said Louise. "Might help the police find Richard's body."

"Good. She went quite a long ways on this logging road. It's a wonder she didn't get stuck on the ruts." Louise was digging through the glove compartment. "If I can find a pencil, I can note how far we go and on what roads." She pulled out a pen and an old sales slip. "Perfect."

"We'll call the police as soon as we find a phone." After a short distance, they emerged from the woods onto a paved road. She stopped. No traffic, but no obvious landmarks either. "I'll turn right here and see where this goes."

Nancy drove cautiously down the lonely two-lane country road. She saw no houses or other cars, just woods and posted signs.

"I don't know this area at all," said Louise, peering through the darkness.

"I like to drive these back roads." Nancy steered the car around a large pothole. "I'm hoping to see something soon that I recognize."

They came to an unmarked crossroads. Nancy cocked an eyebrow at Louise. "Which way, navigator?"

Louise shrugged. Nancy turned left. They rounded a bend and

both heaved a sigh of relief. "I know where we are," Nancy said. She glanced at Louise.

"Almost home," she called out and high-fived Louise's good hand.

"We survived another one," said Louise with a grin.

***

Lecture Series:
The Race to Reckon Longitude
Monday, 7 p.m., Auditorium

Where in the world are you and how do you find out? Ways to determine latitude, the distance north or south of the equator, were relatively simple to develop, but determining longitude, your position east or west, proved more difficult. Not being able to determine longitude cost so many lives and ships that Parliament established a 20,000-pound prize in 1714 for anyone who could devise a way to do it.

Find out more about this fascinating story from Malcolm P. Cook, Ph.D., this month's guest lecturer for Whisperwood's Science Series. Dr. Wagner is professor of mathematics, Morgantown State University. He is the son of Whisperwood resident Mabel T. Cook.

The lecture is free. Refreshments will be served.

- The Whisperwood Breeze, Newsletter for Whisperwood Retirement Village

CHAPTER 33

The 90s Club sat on the hard wooden bleachers in the gymnasium at the local high school. The strains of "Pomp and Circumstance" had begun, and Nancy swallowed to hold back the tears as she always did when she heard that piece of music. Everyone was standing now as the graduates marched down the aisles to take their seats before the podium. Taneesha said she'd be coming down the left-side aisle, and she, Louise, George, and Fitz were all watching for her.

"There she is," yelled Fitz, pointing Taneesha out to the others. They all called her name, George stamped his feet and Louise whistled. Taneesha turned to look and waved, her smile broad and face beaming.

"I am so proud of her," Nancy whispered, finding it hard to speak.

"Me, too," said Louise and she swiped at her eyes. Nancy glanced at her in wonder. Louise who never cried at anything, who scoffed at shows of emotion, was as touched as she was.

After the ceremony, the 90s Club worked their way through the crowd at the reception to congratulate Taneesha. They finally found her, standing with her parents, at a table of cookies and lemonade.

Taneesha made the introductions, and then her Dad cleared his throat. A tall dignified African-American in gray suit and tie, he shook each of their hands solemnly. "Taneesha has told me a lot about you. I can't thank you enough for the opportunity Whisperwood gave my daughter."

Her mother, a thin woman in pantsuit who seemed tense with pent-up energy, came forward. "She's the first one in our family to go to college."

"She won't be the last," her father added. "Thank you for all your support."

Nancy shook her head. "Taneesha is wonderful. We only needed to get out of her way."

"Well, young lady," said George, smiling benignly at Taneesha, "Congratulations and good luck to you. Now I saw some cake around here somewhere." He bowed. "We'll let you celebrate in peace."

Nancy smiled to soften George's words. "I'm sure there are others you want to see here. We are all very proud of Taneesha."

The 90s Club turned to leave, but Taneesha rushed forward to hug Nancy, then she hugged the others in turn. "Thank you," she said, then stepped back to join her parents who were already walking away, having spotted people they knew in the crowd.

"Go get yourself some cake, George," said Louise. "Honestly! As if we didn't get enough to eat."

'Hurry up," added Nancy. "We have another stop to make before heading home."

"Really?" asked Fitz. "Where?"

"We're meeting Geri, Betts' sister, for a late lunch." Nancy checked her watch as she began walking to the parking lot.

Louise nodded as she followed Nancy. "We need to fill her in. She must have questions."

"Yes, but thanks to you and Nancy," Fitz added, "the Whisperwood scammers are out of business." He frowned, staring down at the ground as he walked. "Plenty more out there, though."

"We'll keep up the educational programs," said Louise, "in the computer lab, the newsletter, lectures. The people here won't be fooled again."

Nancy glanced at Louise. "How's your bee petition going?"

"Got a majority of the residents on board," Louise said with satisfaction. "We'll be making changes in the landscaping management, no doubt about it. The new landscaping management committee is all set up."

"She's something, isn't she?" George beamed and put an arm around her and squeezed. Louise blushed and pushed him away.

Nancy retrieved her car and fifteen minutes later, they were seated in a local restaurant in town. Geri had already arrived and sat at a table, watching for them. The restaurant with its light pine walls and red and white tablecloths and curtains looked more like Bavaria than West Virginia. Most of the lunch crowd had left, leaving only a few customers scattered in booths near the windows.

After the initial greetings and the server had taken their orders, Geri folded her arms on the table. "Thank you for finding my sister's killer," she said in a low voice. "You told me a little of what happened, and I understand one of them is dead and the other one severely injured."

"That's right," said Nancy. "The police are still looking for the so-called nephew."

"Tell me the whole story," Geri said, casting her glance at all of them around the table. "I had met Grace, and I am shocked. I don't think my sister liked her very much. I guess Grace was afraid of her."

Their orders arrived at that propitious moment. For a few moments, they busied themselves salting, sugaring and fixing their meals, then Nancy took a sip from her iced tea and began.

Louise, George, and Fitz interrupted again and again with details and insights but in the end, Geri nodded. "You almost lost your lives in that mess. My family owes you a debt of gratitude."

"Oh please," said Louise. "We've had enough gratitude today. Just glad to still be here, that's all."

Nancy set down her sandwich. "There is one thing," she said.

"What is that?" Geri asked.

"You said your whole family knew the secret of Grace's old clock. I would dearly love to know what it is." Nancy sat back and waited.

Geri smiled.

"Yeah, what is it?" Louise asked. "Some kind of code?" Her arms folded, plate empty, and only a sip of iced tea remaining in her glass, she frowned at Geri.

Geri laughed. "I can see you're all eager to know." She looked at Louise. "You might say it was a kind of code."

"But what?" asked Nancy. "I couldn't see anything that could be a cipher or a code either."

"It is serious, though," Geri added. "And it probably saved my family. You see, that clock was used as a signal for the Underground Railroad."

"What?" said Louise and Nancy simultaneously.

"Yes, that's right." Geri smiled at their reaction. "Jefferson would love this story, I'm sure."

George finally spoke. "Just tell us the facts, ma'am."

"I don't know whether Grace or Jefferson's ancestors owned the clock, but the ancestors who had the jewelry store in Richmond put that clock in the store window whenever a conductor was coming to take runaway slaves out of Richmond and over to Fort

Monroe, which was held by the Union army."

"Excuse me," said Fitz. "I'm not getting this. What do you mean by conductor?"

"A conductor was someone who guided runaway slaves to the various stations on the Underground Railroad. That was just a metaphor, you know, meaning the series of safe houses and places that would harbor the runaways. The safe houses were called stations. Get it?"

Nancy nodded. "I see. And someone told me that Fort Monroe, on the coast east of Richmond, was one of the stations."

"That's true." Geri tried to keep her voice light. "My family used that clock to get to the conductor who took them to Fort Monroe. It was right at the mouth of the Chesapeake Bay, where it emptied into the Atlantic. Anyway, from the fort, they managed to board a ship going to Philadelphia. That's where I'm from."

The 90s Club, Nancy, Louise, Fitz and George, sat silently, pondering Geri's story. Finally, Nancy said, "Thank you for giving us the background on that clock. I didn't solve its secret, but now at least I know what it was."

"So what's going to happen to the clock now?" asked George.

Nancy shook her head. "I suppose it will go to Jefferson as next of kin, but I'll tell him the story and suggest he give it to you, Geri."

Louise snorted. "Oh yeah, like that'll happen."

"Tell him the story. I'll bet he'll want to get rid of it," said Geri. "And I propose to buy it."

Nancy nodded. "And that would be a fitting end."

"Almost," said Louise, grinning. "Now we have to get in shape for our excursion to Maine and Nova Scotia. We'll have to get hiking boots and toughen up for the steps and hikes. After all. . ."

She and Nancy finished the sentence together. "There are no accommodations for disabilities."

***

**Auction Set for Saturday,
June 25, 10 a.m.,
Special Events Room**

Heirloom keepsakes, silver, furniture.
Featured item: Henri Marc 18th century 8-day
clock. White porcelain. Minimum bid: $2,000
Items may be viewed
in the auction room at 9 a.m.
Advance catalog will be mailed upon request.
Auctioneer: Buck Wilson, 555-BUCK.

- *Newspaper ad and flyer*

SPECIAL THANKS

RomanceScams.org is an information and advocacy organization established in 2005 to create public awareness and provide accurate information and expertise to assist in terminating online romance scams while providing resources, personal stories, and other assistance to help victims of such scams.

Hampton History Museum offers a fine collection of maps, photographs, and artifacts detailing the history of Hampton, VA. The tour begins in a Kecoughtan Indian longhouse, passes through the hold of a tobacco ship and visits the ruins of the city burned to the ground during the Civil War. Well worth a visit. 120 Old Hampton Lane, Hampton, VA 23669.

Fort Monroe Casement Museum: On an island east of Hampton, VA, this museum is inside the walls of the fort. To enter, you must drive over a moat and through the gate to park inside the fort. The museum is a fascinating—and spooky—place to visit. The fort is an official national monument and is operated by the Commonwealth of Virginia with curatorial support provided by the United States Army.

National Watch and Clock Museum: All ages will find this museum entertaining and educational with exhibits on the history of timekeeping and over 12,000 items including all kinds of clocks. A world-class museum tucked away in a small town between Lancaster and York, Pennsylvania. 121 Poplar Street, Columbia, PA 17512.

If you enjoyed The 90s Club & the Secret of the Old Clock, _you might also enjoy the other books in the series. All available as print and e-books._

The 90s Club & the Hidden Staircase

The 90s Club at Whisperwood Retirement Village discovers a simmering brew of thefts, murders, and exploitation bubbling beneath its luxurious lifestyle. Nancy Dickenson and fellow club members pile up clues like tricks in a bridge game to uncover the culprits—and almost lose their lives. "A must" for readers of cozy mysteries." – *Midwest Book Review.*

The 90s Club & the Whispering Statue

The 90s Club heads to Fort Lauderdale to rescue one friend and search for another. Four attempts to murder club member Nancy's long-time confidant Peter have failed, but in the placid lifestyle of his retirement condo, who would want to kill Peter and why? "A fun read...nostalgia and...social commentary wrapped up in an engaging mystery novel." - *Foreword Reviews*

Also by Eileen Haavik McIntire

Shadow of the Rock

Two women, 200 years apart, seek their past and their future on journeys that will link the old world with the new and change the map of Florida. "A bold adventure." - *Foreword Reviews.* "Highly recommended." *Midwest Book Review.*